End

Jennifer A. Miskov's new book, *Fasting for Fire: Igniting Fresh Hunger to Feast Upon God,* is an important reminder for a new generation about the importance of fasting. Fasting has been a big part of my walk with God and ministry. The gift of fasting is available to us all and will prepare us to step into revival and all that God has for us.

DR. RANDY CLARK
Founder of Global Awakening

I am so grateful that *Fasting for Fire* is coming out in this perfect season. I can see all over the world a polarization of religious people willing to put up more rules while at the same time there is a new generation rising up so hungry and thirsty of a true move of the Holy Spirit.

For many years, I've adopted the very important keys for revival, prayer and fasting, as a lifestyle. I highly appreciate the spirit behind this book in revealing keys and helping every believer with practical steps to allow the volcano of the greatest revival in this history to erupt sooner than we expect.

JEAN-LUC TRACHSEL
President of the International Association
of Healing Ministries (IAHM)

Jen has been a friend and an inspiration to me for years. I have watched her live a consecrated and fasting lifestyle not just from the stage, but behind closed doors when no one was watching.

It was by Jen's leading that I began to fast consistently and see the power of fasting for myself. For Jen, the pursuit of Jesus and consecration to Him are not just temporary trends, another desire among many others, or a book topic, these two things have been driving forces in her public and private life for many years. Her love, passion, and dedication for Jesus has continually inspired me and many others.

I truly believe that as you read *Fasting for Fire*, it will not just teach you, although it will do that, it will not just inspire you, though it will also do that, but I truly believe as you read though this book, you will receive impartation from Jen and these other heroes. I pray that you will receive an impartation of ravenous hunger for Him and Him alone. I pray that as you read these words, the revelation will come that there is literally nothing and no one else that will satisfy like He does. I pray that as you fast, you will be filled by Him.

JESSIKA TATE
Founder/President Yielded Ministries Global

Dr. Miskov's book *Fasting for Fire* is a much-needed reminder and an in-depth teaching on a powerful tool for breakthrough found in fasting. I'm a firm believer in fasting and have found it to be the main driver of seeing heavenly purposes released in earthen vessels. The truths and concepts revealed in these pages will ignite a spiritual hunger in your heart and set you on a relentless pursuit of the Eternal One.

TEOFILO HAYASHI
Founder Dunamis Movement

As you journey through the pages of this powerful book, you will learn the ways of the Burning Ones. These are the laid-down Lovers of Jesus who changed history.

Each wisdom key Jen shares in *Fasting for Fire* provides us with a doorway into the deeper supernatural life of true intimacy with Jesus. I truly believe your life is about to radically change. This is your moment.

LIZ WRIGHT

Founding Director Liz Wright Ministries

International Bestselling Author of *Reflecting God: Spiritual Keys to Unlock the Supernatural You*

The ways of the kingdom of God are counter to the ways of the world. Those who exalt themselves will be brought down, but those who humble themselves will be exalted. Those who seek to save their lives will lose them, but those who lose their lives for Christ will save them. In regard to fasting, those who are always full will become empty, but those who are sometimes empty will become full of God. Jennifer Miskov's book, *Fasting for Fire: Igniting Fresh Hunger to Feast Upon God*, is an urgent and encouraging reminder that those who hunger and thirst shall be filled! Packed with powerful testimonies, this book will take you into a new dimension of intimacy with God. Read Jen's book, then follow her example. You will not be disappointed.

LEE ROY MARTIN, PH.D.

Professor of Old Testament and Biblical Languages

Pentecostal Theological Seminary

Cleveland, Tennessee

Fasting for Fire is a supernatural invitation to feast on the presence of God. This book is page after page of impartation. You will find yourself wanting to fast after receiving a clear vision of what fasting will usher you into.

LARRY SPARKS
Publisher
Destiny Image

I can't wait for this book to be in the hands of every believer! We need less social media opinions and more praying, more fasting, and more consecrated ones! Spiritual disciplines are so often lost in today's culture, as many of us have taken the bait from the deceiver and pendulum swung into fear of "legalism" and have completely dismissed this pure invitation for increased intimacy.

I can earnestly say that I would not be leading revival without fasting. This book that Jen has written is so timely! *Fasting for Fire!* We say "Yes! God!"

I believe the remnant that the Lord has called and anointed in this hour will be those who fast and pray. I urge you, pick up this book, practice what it says, and step into the fire!

JESSI GREEN
Author of *Wildfires*
Revivalist—Saturate Global

I wholeheartedly endorse Jen's book, *Fasting for Fire*, as she presents the truths about fasting in such a balanced, scriptural, and life-giving way. The heart of this book is centered upon Jesus and the Holy Spirit and will draw you closer to God. I trust that this book will help all of us in our daily journey with Him and in reaching the lost for the kingdom and for His glory.

MEL TARI
Author of *Like a Mighty Wind*

Fasting *for* Fire

Igniting Fresh Hunger to Feast Upon God

Jennifer A. Miskov, Ph.D.

with Randy Clark and Lou Engle

DESTINY IMAGE® PUBLISHERS, INC.

P.O. Box 310, Shippensburg, PA 17257-0310

"Promoting Inspired Lives."

This book and all other Destiny Image and Destiny Image Fiction books are available at Christian bookstores and distributors worldwide.

Cover design by Eileen Rockwell

Interior design by Terry Clifton

For more information on foreign distributors, call 717-532-3040.

Reach us on the Internet: www.destinyimage.com.

ISBN 13 TP: 978-0-7684-5949-4

ISBN 13 eBook: 978-0-7684-5950-0

ISBN 13 HC: 978-0-7684-5952-4

ISBN 13 LP: 978-0-7684-5951-7

For Worldwide Distribution, Printed in the U.S.A.

2 3 4 5 6 7 8 / 25 24 23 22

I dedicate this book to Lou Engle.

I know of no greater mobilizer of fasters and Nazirites in our generation than you. You have paved the way for us all.

Generations will ride on the momentum you have laid down your life for us to step into.

I am so grateful that my spiritual mother in the faith, Carrie Judd Montgomery, and your spiritual father in the faith, Frank Bartleman, were friends over a century ago. What a privilege it was to first meet you in Oakland at a well of revival called the Home of Peace I discovered in my studies.

I pray that this offering on fasting will honor you and demonstrate that your legacy of being a burning one will be multiplied and continue far beyond what you could ever hope, dream, or imagine.

Contents

Foreword *by Heidi Baker* 1

Introduction 7

Chapter 1   Foundations in Fire 9

Chapter 2   Testimonies of Fasting Revivalists 15

Chapter 3   Revival of the Disciplines 27

Chapter 4   Feasting Upon God 37

Chapter 5   Motivations for Fasting 47

Chapter 6   The Bridegroom Fast *by Lou Engle* 55

Chapter 7   God's Chosen Fast *by Randy Clark* 63

Chapter 8   To Obey Is Better Than Sacrifice
            (with Heidi Baker) 69

Chapter 9   Practical Tips 79

Chapter 10 Longer Fasts *(with Heidi Baker)* 89

Chapter 11 Corporate Fasts 99

Chapter 12 Breakthroughs in Fasting *by Lou Engle* 111

Chapter 13 Dreams and Revelation *by Lou Engle* 117

Chapter 14 A Spirit of Burning 123

Chapter 15 Tend to the Inward Fire *by Lou Engle* 133

Chapter 16 The Fire Fast 139

Chapter 17 Impartation 153

Chapter 18   Activation 1: The Fire Fast of Intimacy......161

Chapter 19   Activation 2: The Fire Fast of Consecration .167

Chapter 20   Activation 3: The Fire Fast of Revival 173

Chapter 21   Bonus Activation 4: The Fire Fast of Destiny..177

Chapter 22   Bonus Tips *by Lou Engle*....................183

             Further Resources........................191

Foreword
by Heidi Baker

I am so thankful to the Lord for the different ways He calls us to fast and to push away from the world to get closer to Him. Fasting brings us to the place where we are focused on Jesus and can press in for more of Him. When we fast, we put the armor of God on and connect with Him in a deeper way. It sharpens us in many ways.

Whether you fast from food or from media, fast in a way where you are *hungry* just for Jesus. *Eating and drinking of Jesus is the most important part of fasting. He* is the bread of life. *He* is the drink. In fasting, we spend that extra time getting nourished in Him. It is absolutely beautiful.

Over the last twenty-four years since I've traveled the world to one hundred and thirty nations, I've seen so many people get touched by Holy Spirit. I've seen them run forward and say "yes" to fasting, "yes" to missions, "yes" to serving the Lord around the world. But when the costs come in, when it's time to buy that ticket, when it's time to say "no" to a relationship that they believed the Lord was giving to them, sometimes people don't follow through.

I remember when the Lord told me to break up with my fiancé six weeks before my wedding. Those kinds of "yeses" to the Lord are what literally will mark your life; those are costly. The Lord doesn't just ask you to follow through when the fire of God is falling and His presence is crashing in on you. He says, "Follow through even when you don't feel like it. Follow through even when it is challenging."

For me, fasting is not my most favorite thing to do if I am honest. But I know the result of it is powerful, because in fasting God cuts away everything that doesn't bring Him pleasure. When we're fasting and getting away with God, He cuts away, through His Word, the things that need to be cut away in our lives. Fasting is especially powerful for the pruning process of getting rid of everything Jesus knows will hold us back. In fasting, if the Father wants to get rid of something, He just chops. He removes anything and everything that would hinder us from all that He has.

I want to pray for you as you begin to go on this journey into greater intimacy with Jesus by reading Fasting for Fire.

Lord, right now I ask as each one fasts, as they feast on You and seek Your face, that You would prune them. Let every fruitful branch yield a greater harvest. Lord, clean each one and prune each one.

Jesus says in John 15:4–8:

So you must remain in life-union with me, for I remain in life-union with you. For as a branch severed from the vine will not bear fruit, so your life will be fruitless unless you live your life intimately joined to mine. I am the sprouting vine and you're my branches. As you live in union with me as your source, fruitfulness will stream from within you—but when you live separated from me you are powerless. If a person is separated from me, he is discarded; such branches are gathered up and thrown into the fire to be burned. But if you live in life-union with me and if my words live powerfully within you—then you can ask whatever you desire and it will be done. When your lives bear abundant fruit, you demonstrate that you are my mature disciples who glorify my Father! (TPT)

Lord, I ask that You burn away every distraction in each one as they fast, as they feast upon You, and as they worship. Burn away everything that doesn't bring You pleasure. Cut it away so they will be ignited by Your passionate love. Let their lives bear much fruit. Thank You, Jesus. Amen.

Lover of God, I want to encourage you as you step into fasting and into greater feasting with the Lord. As you feast upon the beauty of Jesus and eat and drink of Him, may greater explosive power flow through you as you obey this wooing. There is great joy in nourishing yourself on the Lord Himself and on His Word. I pray as you step into this journey with fasting to feast upon the Lord that you understand *the joy* of abiding in the vine. I pray that He uses the anointing on *Fasting for Fire* and the message He has put in Jen's heart to touch your life in a powerful way. I pray that God would flood you right now and pour out His presence and glory over you in a radical way as you say "yes" to drawing closer to His heart.

HEIDI BAKER, PH.D.
Founding Director, Iris Global

Unrelenting Fire

Fasten me upon your heart
as a seal of fire forevermore.
This living, consuming flame
will seal you as my prisoner of love.
My passion is stronger
than the chains of death and the grave,
all consuming as the very flashes of fire
from the burning heart of God.
Place this fierce, unrelenting
fire over your entire being.
Rivers of pain and persecution
will never extinguish this flame.
Endless floods will be unable
to quench this raging fire that burns within you.
Everything will be consumed.
It will stop at nothing
as you yield everything to this furious fire
until it won't even seem to
you like a sacrifice anymore.
—Song of Songs 8:6–7 (TPT)

Introduction

This book is for the lovers.

If you are reading this right now, that is you. I believe the Holy Spirit has orchestrated this moment to place this book into your hands because you are a burning one who has experienced the radical love of Jesus and are compelled to give Him everything in return.

This book is not for the religious ones who have it all together or for those who like to brag about what they can "accomplish" for Christ. This book is for the courageous ones who live from their hearts even if it looks messy at times. It's for those who are not afraid to take risks, and even to fail at times, and who have the determination and resilience to get back up and try again. It's for those who have been radically marked by the love of God and are hungry to know Him more. It's for those who have encountered His goodness and know that He alone satisfies. This book is for those who will do anything to be closer to Him and are willing to pay any price to know His heart.

In this little handbook, I share testimonies of fasting revivalists, why it is important to fast, motivations for fasting, practical tips, and personal experiences with fasting. I also invited a few special mothers and fathers in the faith I know to share about their experiences with fasting. Additionally, I introduce a revolutionary perspective on fasting called the Fire Fast where you will learn about the Fire Fast of Intimacy, the Fire Fast of Consecration, and the Fire Fast of Revival, as well as have the opportunity to be activated in these.

As you read *Fasting for Fire*, may the fire of first love be reignited in your heart. As you go on this journey with me in exploring the hidden treasure of fasting, may it whet your appetite to feast upon the living God in a greater way. May the gift of increased hunger be imparted to you. I pray that God would break you free from any religious boxes or mindsets holding you back from freely accessing this invitation for more of Him. I pray that a burning passion for Jesus would be catalyzed and you would encounter the love of the Father like never before.

Let the adventure begin!

CHAPTER 1

Foundations in Fire

*My recommendation for the Christian church
today is to call a moratorium on all activity and
focus on coming into worship until the fire descends
and engulfs us in the sacredness of His presence.*[1]

—A. W. TOZER

Fire

Burning ones fast and fasting ones burn.

Fasting and fire are inseparable. There is something about fasting that ignites an all-consuming fire for God inside. Fire brings us to a place of intense focus. Fire can also represent passionate, burning love. No other lovers can compete for our attention when we are captivated, on fire, and intently focused on the face of Jesus.

Hebrews 12:29 says that our God "is a consuming fire." Choosing to live in the fire is essentially embracing the fiery presence of God Himself. When doing this continuously, there is a unique purity and consecration that happens. In the fire, everything must be purified and refined like gold. There is a respect for the holiness of God by welcoming a life refined by the fire.[2]

Fire can also represent revival. If we define one element of revival as simply being more in love with Jesus and completely yielded for His purposes, then as we focus our gaze upon the fire in His eyes, signs, wonders, and miracles are sure to follow. We don't need to strive for revival to be released through our lives when our hearts burn for the One Thing more than any other lover. Revival is something that will naturally flow from the fire of God's presence in our lives and our intimate communion with Him.

Resurgence of Fasting

Fasting for Fire: Igniting Fresh Hunger to Feast Upon God originally came from a blog I wrote in 2014 entitled "Fasting: The Lost Art of Feasting Upon God." Interestingly enough, this has been one of my most frequented blogs. This surprised me. I always loved fasting, but to realize others were also interested was a fascinating discovery. Because I have experienced God in powerful ways as I have adopted a lifestyle of fasting,

I want to share more about this pathway to intimacy and show how easily accessible it is no matter one's starting point.

We are alive at such a unique time in history when God is bringing in one of the greatest harvests of souls we've ever known. So many people will be entering into the family of God in this new season. How amazing would it be if, when people entered into the kingdom of God, they also embraced a lifestyle of fasting that was marked by intimacy, consecration, and revival from the very start?

Unfortunately, many Christians have yet to discover or embrace the gift of fasting in our day. But what if fasting were not something exceptional in our generation? What would happen if spiritual fasting became a *regular* part of the Christian life rather than something reserved only for the religious elite? Or better yet, what if fasting for fire became the norm? I wonder what deeper levels of union with Jesus and profound revelation of the Holy Spirit might be tapped into when more believers access this pathway to intimacy. What type of deeper communion, extraordinary miracles, mass salvations, defining moments, increased anointing, and power might be released when the body of Christ strengthens her muscles in this way? How many more revival fires might be ignited when a community of burning ones gathers together, praying and fasting to take hold of more of God?

When a generation embraces the fire of God by setting themselves apart to fast, we will see an unstoppable army of lovers running hard after Him regardless of the cost. These fiery, consecrated, and set-apart saints will turn the world upside down for His glory. And fasting will be one of the pathways to increase and sustain their flame of love for Jesus.

Hunger

In my studies of revival history over the last several decades, *the number-one attribute that is present in the beginnings of almost every revival I've looked at is hunger.* I discovered that hunger was the strongest component that initially stirred people to pray, position themselves, press in, and be desperate for a move of God. This hunger was first stirred up in their own lives, which later became catalytic for everyone around them.

So, if hunger for more of God is one of the most prominent elements God has used in history to catalyze revivals, wouldn't it be amazing if there was a way for us to cultivate greater hunger for God today?

What if I told you that there is something very practical you can do today to cultivate increased hunger for God? Or that there is something you can integrate into your lifestyle that will radically accelerate your spiritual growth? Well, I have good news for you. There is! Fasting done with the right motives is one sure way to grow your hunger for God and access deeper levels of intimacy with Him. Besides asking God to give you the gift of hunger, you can also choose to embrace a lifestyle of fasting to grow your hunger for Him. A lifestyle of fasting can also contribute to greater anointing and power working through your life as you continue to yield to the Holy Spirit.

Jesus

Let me just say from the start that fasting is not the answer.

Jesus is the answer.

Fasting is not a formula to get God to do what we want. Fasting is simply one of the gifts or pathways to intimacy given to us that can help accelerate our growth in Christ and lead us into deeper union with Him. If signs, wonders, and miracles follow times of fasting, that's amazing. However, that is not the focus of our fasting or our end game here. The point of fasting for fire is to get more of Jesus and allow Him to get more of us. Fasting is simply an invitation to know God more. It is all for Jesus. It must begin in Him, find its source in Him, and end with more of Him. In all of our fastings, may we get more of Jesus as our reward.

Notes

1. A. W. Tozer, *The Fire of God's Presence: Drawing Near to a Holy God* edited by James L. Snyder (Minneapolis, MN: Bethany House, 2020), 41.
2. See Leviticus 6:8–13; Matthew 3:11; Romans 12:1–2.

CHAPTER 2

Testimonies of Fasting Revivalists

I would rather have a man on my platform not filled with the Holy Ghost but hungry for God, than a man who has received the Holy Ghost but has become satisfied with his experience.[1]

—SMITH WIGGLESWORTH

Testimonies Prophesy

Testimonies remind us of what God has done in the past and give us prophetic vision for what He can and wants to do again in our day. As we begin this journey together, let's first explore what God has done in history so we can then ask Him to do it again in an even greater measure in our lives today.

Many of the great revivalists we look up to have one thing in common: they regularly incorporated fasting into their rhythm of life. Many have even done forty-day fasts. Interestingly enough, many defining moments, life callings, and even revival movements have been initiated when people were on a fast. Cultivating hunger for God through fasting is one of the most consistent characteristics that precede and catalyze revivals. *Hunger for more of God* is a common denominator in the ignition of most revival fires.

Throughout history, countless times, hunger is stirred in people for more of God, so they go on a fast to encounter more of Him. In the process, God crashes in to mark them in a profound way and sometimes even a revival movement is birthed. Besides heroes found in the Bible like Moses, David, Elijah, Esther, Daniel, Anna, Paul, Peter, John the Baptist, and Jesus Himself, here are a few testimonies of how some of our other heroes of the faith regularly fasted and the impact it had on their lives and communities.

John Wesley (1703–1791) and his community formed a group they called the Holy Club. They fasted two different days every week together as a community, training themselves to walk in the fullness of all that God had for them in their generation. They also regularly gave to the poor. Wesley was a part of birthing both the First Great Awakening and the Methodist movement that came from it. The YWAM ministry called Circuit Riders was inspired from Wesley's original circuit rider evangelists.

Charles Finney (1792–1875) prepared for revivals by organizing teams to pray, fast, and spread the word before he arrived. His prayer warrior, Daniel Nash, went into towns before him for a few weeks or even months to pray, fast, and prepare the fallow ground for the seeds that were about to be sown. Finney, who pioneered the altar call and became known as the Father of Modern Revivalism, played a significant role in the Second Great Awakening.

Smith Wigglesworth (1859–1947) was a powerful healing evangelist within the Pentecostal movement. Immediately following a turning point in his marriage, which included a deep conviction to turn back to God, Wigglesworth decided to go on a ten-day fast to get his heart right. During this set-apart time of consecration unto the Lord, there was a marked change in him. His temper and moodiness left. He was a different man.[2]

Wigglesworth, who moved in great anointing and healing power, fasted and prayed one day each week for fifty souls to be saved on Sunday. He never remembered "seeing less than fifty souls saved by the power of God in the meetings with the children, in the hospitals, on the ships, and in the Salvation Army."[3]

One fun story of how God moved through Wigglesworth's lifestyle of prayer and fasting happened when he received a telegram to pray for a dangerously ill boy in England. Once he arrived in the town, his determination to see the boy's healing caused him to go another nine miles on bicycle to get to the farm where the boy lay. When he arrived, the boy's mother told him it was too late because her son was nearly dead. Wigglesworth told her that God never sent him anywhere too late. He prayed and fasted and then asked the parents to dry the boy's clothes so they would be ready to put on. Wigglesworth then went off to church where he was asked to preach. He came back to find that the parents had not done as he asked. He went and got the clothes and had someone put the boy's stockings on him. Then he asked everyone to leave the room and he shut the door behind him.

When he began to pray and touched the boy's hand, the power of God invaded the room and knocked Wigglesworth to the floor. He lay there in the glory for over fifteen minutes. During this time, the boy regained his strength so much that he shouted for joy. After the boy dressed, he ran to tell his parents the great news but found them knocked over on the floor in the kitchen as a result of the glory that filled the house. "The daughter who had been brought from the asylum and whose mind was still affected was made perfectly whole that day. That whole village was moved and a revival began that day."[4]

Rees Howells (1879–1950) was used by God to help steward the fire from the Welsh Revival (1904–1905) through discipleship. Following his defining moment that came as a result of extreme and absolute surrender, Howells embraced a lifestyle of consecration. During one season of his life, he fasted two meals a day. During this time, he also spent three hours every night on his knees from 6:00–9:00 p.m., two hours reading the Bible, and one hour of waiting on God. About this precious time of prayer and fasting, Howells recalls:

> Although we may be away from the presence of people, how hard it is to silence the voices of self. But after a time the Lord brought me to the place where the moment I shut the door at six o'clock, I left the world outside and had access into the presence of God.[5]

When the Welsh Revival brought in over 100,000 souls in less than six months, Howells had a burden from the Lord to build a discipleship school so that none of the newly converted believers would be lost. With less than a dollar to his name, he stepped out in faith and founded the Bible College of Wales, where fasting became a practice that was embedded into the foundations of the school.

William J. Seymour (1870–1922) was on a ten-day fast when he preached in a little house on Bonnie

Brae Street in Los Angeles on April 9, 1906. While he was preaching on Acts 2, the Holy Spirit crashed in and marked people with revival fire and a fresh baptism of the Spirit with speaking in tongues. Less than a week later, they moved into a larger building on Azusa Street. This marked the beginnings of the Azusa Street Revival, which in turn helped birth and spread Pentecostalism around the world. This move of God is known as one of the most significant revivals the world has ever known and continues to gain momentum and impact people over a century later. This revival movement was birthed while Seymour and some of his friends were on a ten-day fast, gathering together to call out to God for a fresh baptism of the Holy Spirit.[6]

John G. Lake (1870–1935) was a healing evangelist who pioneered healing rooms and saw many miracles in his ministry. He embraced a focused rhythm of prayer and fasting for nine months while he waited to receive his Pentecostal Spirit baptism experience. Lake was praying with a friend for a sick woman when the Holy Spirit possessed Lake afresh like lightning, and he received his Spirit baptism experience and spoke in tongues. What he had been laboring for in prayer and fasting for nine months had finally come to pass. He didn't pray once and then stop. He prayed through until he experienced what he had set his heart on.

Aimee Semple McPherson (1890–1944) was the first person to utilize the radio as a healing evangelist. At one point in her life, she was so desperate for more of God that she told Him the following:

> Oh, Lord, I am so hungry for your Holy Spirit. You have told me that in the day when I seek with my whole heart you will be found by me. Now Lord, I am going to stay right here until you pour out upon me the promise of the Holy Spirit for whom you commanded me to tarry, if I die of starvation. I am so hungry for Him I can't wait another day. I will not eat another meal until you baptize me.[7]

Not long after she prayed this, she was baptized in the Spirit and continued to be used by God in a significant way in her generation and beyond. She went on to establish the Foursquare movement, which continues to have a global impact to this day. She also pioneered new ways to present the Gospel to her generation through media and the creative arts. During the Great Depression, she fed more people in Los Angeles than the Red Cross.

Randy Clark (1952–present), a one-time Baptist minister, had a series of prophetic words and impartations during long seasons of fasting that radically marked his life and shifted the trajectory of his ministry. These encounters prepared him for what would prove to be the launching point for his international ministry in 1994—the Toronto Blessing. He is known to have gone on two forty-day fasts as well as other smaller fasts that preceded great break-throughs in his life. He currently travels the globe and has an expansive healing and equipping ministry.

Lou Engle (1952–present) is a spiritual father in our lifetime who has embraced a lifestyle of fasting and has inspired a generation to be consecrated for His glory. He is greatly influenced by intercessor Frank Bartleman (1871–1936) who helped prepare the way for the Azusa Street Revival through prayer and fasting. Lou has mobilized hundreds of thousands of people to embrace a Nazirite vow of being set apart for God's purposes through prayer and fasting. His Azusa Now stadium event on the 110-year anniversary of the Azusa Street Revival was birthed during a fast. You will hear from him firsthand in relation to his experiences with fasting in several upcoming chapters in this book.

Heidi Baker (1959–present) is a missionary from Laguna Beach, California, who, along with her husband, Rolland, has been used of God to see the nation of Mozambique transformed through the love of Jesus. Heidi embraced a lifestyle of fasting even from a young age. A few months after her conversion, while on a five-day fast, she attended a little Pentecostal church and went up to the altar. When she knelt down and lifted her arms up to heaven, she was caught up in a vision where God's glory wrapped around her in a bright light. She was overwhelmed in the presence of God and then heard Him speak audibly to her, calling her to be a missionary to Africa, England, and Asia.[8] This vision she received while on a fast informed and shaped the rest of her life. Even today, Heidi encourages her pastoral team and all of her leaders to embrace a rhythm of fasting one day a week together.

Rhythms

All of the revivalists mentioned in this chapter had or have a close relationship with God and a powerful ministry. They also all have one thing in common: they fasted at different times in their lives or regularly integrated fasting into their rhythm of life to grow in their hunger for more of God. For some, their time of fasting was preparation and preceded defining moments in their personal lives. Following their personal awakenings, great outpourings in their ministries or global revival movements were then birthed. For others, fasting was simply a discipline of remaining full of the Holy Spirit and tapping into their longing for more of Jesus. Still others experienced life-defining calls, increased power and anointing in their ministry, and greater intimacy with the Lord. All of these revivalists made fasting a regular part of their rhythm with God. We can follow in their footsteps to ride on the momentum they set before us.

Notes

1. W. Hacking, *Smith Wigglesworth Remembered* (Tulsa, OK: Harrison House Publishers, Inc., 1981), 29–30.
2. Smith Wigglesworth, *Faith That Prevails* (Springfield, MO: Gospel Publishing House, 1938, 1966), 61.
3. Stanley Howard Frodsham, *Smith Wigglesworth: Apostle of Faith* (London: Elim Publishing Co., Ltd., 1949), 5–6.
4. Ibid., 30–31.
5. Norman P. Grubb, *Rees Howells: Intercessor* (Fort Washington, PA: CLC Publications, 2008 reprint from 1952), 114.
6. Jennifer A. Miskov, *Ignite Azusa: Positioning for a New Jesus Revolution* (Redding, CA: Silver to Gold, 2016).
7. Aimee Semple McPherson, *This Is That: Personal Experiences, Sermons and Writings of Aimee Semple McPherson* (Los Angeles, CA: The Bridal Call Publishing House, 1919), 43–52.
8. Rolland and Heidi Baker, *There's Always Enough* (England: Sovereign World Ltd., 2003), 23–27. "In May toward the end of the semester I went on a five-day fast to find out more from God about what to do with my life. On the night of the fifth day I expectantly went to the Roarks' little Pentecostal church in the country and was drawn to the altar. I knelt down and lifted my arms to the Lord… Suddenly I felt taken to a new heavenly place. Pastor Roark was preaching, but I couldn't hear his loud, powerful voice

at all. God's glory came to me again, wrapping me in a pure and brilliant white light. I was overwhelmed by who He is. I had never felt so loved, and I began to weep. This time He spoke to me audibly. 'I am calling you to be a minister and a missionary,' He said. 'You are to go to Africa, Asia and England.' Again my heart was pounding and racing. I thought I might die."

CHAPTER 3

Revival of the Disciplines

I have only to wait for the fire. I have built the altar, and laid the wood in order, and have prepared the offering; I have only to wait for the fire.[1]

—EVAN ROBERTS, leader of
the Welsh Revival (1904–05)

Positioning Ourselves to Feast upon God

When I hear people say they want to be like John Wesley, Smith Wigglesworth, John G. Lake, Aimee Semple McPherson, Heidi Baker, or even Jesus, I encourage them to follow in the same footsteps as these spiritual giants and embrace the lifestyle they modeled. All of these welcomed the grace offered to us for deeper intimacy with Jesus found in the spiritual disciplines. They all lived with their lamps full of oil and regularly positioned themselves to step into all that God had by integrating these spiritual rhythms into their daily lives.

All of these also practiced a lifestyle of intentionally building their relationship with Christ through fasting. They were willing to pay a price to walk in holiness. If we want to walk in the same authority, dominion, power, love, and intimacy as these, a good place to start is to tap into the spiritual pathways where they found life.

Before we dive into fasting, let's first set the stage in understanding why the spiritual disciplines are essential to a burning lifestyle. I know many hear the word *discipline* today and cringe. Because of previous experiences or being misguided by religious rules, that word can carry negative connotations. But rather than something that is forced upon us, I want to reframe this language for our purposes. I would like to take it out of the religious box and place it into a *relational* context.

It is important to understand that ultimately, spiritual disciplines are for the purpose of *knowing God*. They are spiritual pathways to deeper intimacy with God. We practice these ways of life by choice, not because we fear punishment or to check off religious boxes. When we are so undone by the love of Jesus, it is easy to receive the invitation to walk on the highway of holiness. The spiritual disciplines help us hold our focus on the face of Jesus through all storms. These are not practiced out of duty but for the sake of feasting upon God in a greater way.

God wants to raise up His bride to embrace all that He has in this new season. He wants to equip us to bring a resurgence of what has been overlooked, forgotten, abused, broken, misunderstood, or misappropriated in the past. God is raising up an army of lovers who will go anywhere and do anything for Him.

Spiritual Pathways to Intimacy

Spiritual disciplines, also known as graces or pathways to intimacy, include prayer, meditation, fasting, feasting, reading the Word, worship, keeping the Sabbath, silence, giving, community, and more. These practices help us to align our lives with heaven and position ourselves to go deeper in our relationship with God. These pathways are an *invitation* to explore the hidden crevices of the Father's heart.

The world is crying out for a deep people who can live from a place of interwovenness with the Creator. These graces of the spiritual life help us become deep people, sourced in the One who is the Living Water of Life.[2] There is so much more of the Father's heart to explore. These pathways simply help take us on that journey.

We tap into the spiritual disciplines so that we can live deep within the heart of God. In his book *Celebration of Discipline*, Richard Foster says, "The desperate need today is not for a greater number of intelligent people, or gifted people, but for deep people."[3] He goes on to say:

> The purpose of the Disciplines is liberation from the stifling slavery to self-interest and fear. When the inner spirit is liberated from all that weighs it down, it can hardly be described as dull drudgery. Singing, dancing, even shouting characterize the Disciplines of the spiritual life![4]

Everyone connects with God differently according to their personality and how they are wired. Some people connect with God in nature or in silence, while others connect with Him during activity or through music or dance. Practicing the disciplines helps everyone, regardless of how they are wired, tap into a greater measure of the heart of God.

I regularly get out in nature to spend time waiting on God, reading His Word, or simply being present with Him. I long to be with Him alone. No one else and nothing else can ever satisfy. Choosing to adopt these spiritual pathways will help position us to be with the One we love. Dedicating time with the living God for the sole purpose of

communing with Him is one of the most valuable invest-
ments we can make in this life.

Embracing the Spiritual Disciplines

- Positions us to hear God's voice
- Deepens our connection with God
- Invites us to feast upon God
- Increases our hunger for more of God
- Aligns us to receive God's blessings
- Prepares us to steward the calling of God on
  our lives
- Helps us keep our lamps full of the oil of the
  Holy Spirit

The spiritual disciplines are intended to bring freedom
and liberation. Our motivation in integrating these should
always be a longing to know God more (see Psalm 42:1–2).
Embracing these pathways to intimacy will bring focus,
self-control, and pave the way to walk on the highway of
holiness. These graces can also act as a purifying fire. It is
the pure in heart who see God (Matthew 5:8). While there
is always the danger of spiritual disciplines degenerating
into law and empty ritualistic practice, fear of this happening should not be greater than the drive to take hold of
the King of kings by positioning ourselves in front of His
throne. The disciplines help us do just that.

Some people confuse the disciplines with striving or trying to manipulate or control God when in reality that could not be further from the truth. While only God can grow us spiritually, there are things we can do to prepare and cultivate our lives to invite this. One helpful way to understand spiritual disciplines is likening them to farming. A farmer can cultivate the ground, plant seeds, water the crops, and create an environment that invites this growth, but he cannot make the seeds grow. However, when the sun shines and the rains come, saturating what has been cultivated, life springs forth (Galatians 5:22–25).

The same is true for us. We all have seeds of destiny God has planted within our hearts. As we tend to the soil of our hearts by practicing the disciplines, we are essentially positioning ourselves under the waterfall of God's grace. The floods of His Holy Spirit saturate our lives, causing the seeds He has planted to spring forth in due time (Isaiah 61:11).

Spiritual disciplines can also be likened to training for sports. Athletes do not win gold medals by sitting at home and watching television. They train their bodies for the big race whether they feel like it or not. Similarly, spiritual disciplines can act as spiritual training for us to be ready to advance the kingdom of God and partner with heaven in season and out. When we have been building our spiritual muscles in this way, we will be ready to set the oppressed free, tear down demonic strongholds, release healing, stop for the one, and love the broken when the time arises (see Jeremiah 1:10). When we have been regularly filling our lamps with oil, we will be ready to join the Bridegroom at the appointed time for the feast He has set before us.

Freedom to Soar in His Presence

If you have been under an oppressive system of law rather than love or have shied away from the spiritual disciplines because you have been wounded by an inappropriate or legalistic implementation of them, on behalf of those who hurt you, I want to say I am so sorry. You shouldn't have been treated that way. I want to ask forgiveness on behalf of any leader who wounded you or misrepresented the joy of the spiritual disciplines.

And I have good news for you. Today is a new day. It is a day of freedom. I am here to introduce a better way. I invite you to be led by the Holy Spirit rather than react to a spirit of fear or false expectation that was put upon you.

God wants time with you. It takes discipline to set aside and guard time for Him alone. You will have to fight a million battles to protect your time with God. The spiritual disciplines will help you win those battles. The disciplines are not intended to imprison you but instead to bind you to Christ Himself. Remember, in their truest form, they are simply pathways to greater intimacy with God.

May God use these grace portals to free you to fully explore and dive deeper into His heart. May accessing these currents of intimacy help position you for greater union with God. Motivated by your love relationship with Jesus and by following the leading of the Spirit, I release you from fear in Jesus' name to embrace these spiritual strengths. I release grace to forgive those who have hurt you through legalism. I impart courage to you to dive into a new world of forsaking all other lovers to embrace Him. Today, I compel you to set everything aside for the sole purpose of beholding Jesus.

> *Here's the one thing I crave from God,*
> *the one thing I seek above all else:*
> *I want the privilege of living with him every moment in his house,*
> *finding the sweet loveliness of his face,*
> *filled with awe, delighting in his glory and grace.*
> *I want to live my life so close to him*
> *that he takes pleasure in my every prayer.*
> (Psalm 27:4 TPT)

Notes

1. "Mr Roberts Tells the Story of His Conversion," *The Religious Revival in Wales*: Contemporary newspaper accounts of the Welsh Revival of 1904–1905 published by the *Western Mail* (Shropshire, England: Quinta Press,

2004), 216–220. This was in a letter from Roberts to Rev. Thomas Francis, a Calvinistic Methodist minister, and dated December 28, 1904.

2. Richard Foster, *Celebration of Discipline* (New York, NY: HarperOne, 1978, reprint 1998), 1–2. Foster says, "The classical Disciplines of the spiritual life call us to move beyond surface living into the depths."

3. Ibid.

4. Ibid.

CHAPTER 4

Feasting Upon God

Listen! Are you thirsty for more?
Come to the refreshing waters and drink.
Even if you have no money,
come, buy, and eat.
Yes, come and buy all the
wine and milk you desire—
it won't cost a thing.
Why spend your hard-earned money
on something that can't nourish you
or work so hard for something that can't satisfy?
So listen carefully to me
and you'll enjoy a sumptuous feast,
delighting in the finest of food.
—Isaiah 55:1–2 (TPT)

What Is Spiritual Fasting?

Now that we have seen the value of embracing spiritual disciplines as a whole, it is time to focus in on the spiritual discipline of fasting. Before I introduce the Fire Fast, let's look at the basics of spiritual fasting and what it is. Spiritual fasting is going without food to cultivate spiritual hunger for God. The fasting that we will be talking about is abstaining from food for spiritual purposes. The purpose of spiritual fasting is to replace food with prayer and communion with God. Whenever one feels a hunger pain, that is a reminder to pray and press into God.

Fasting is really all about feasting upon God. It is a way to accelerate our walk with Him. It is an invitation to greater levels of intimacy. It is also a powerful weapon we can use to tear down strongholds, set the oppressed free, heal the sick, align destinies, and stir up hunger for more of God. In all of the spiritual disciplines, including fasting, our motives should be to seek the face of Jesus above all else (Joel 2:12; Zechariah 7:5; Acts 13:2).

Though fasting is not explicitly stated as a commandment in the Bible, this is likely because most believers already fasted as a regular part of their spirituality. There seems to be an assumption in Scripture that if people were followers of Jesus, then they regularly fasted because He fasted. In a similar way in which Jesus said, "when you give to the needy," implying that was normal and an expected part of spirituality, Jesus also said in Matthew 6:16, "*When* you fast." He did not say "*if*" you fast. If Jesus is our model and He regularly fasted, then we ought to follow in His footsteps.

The Gospels record a time when Jesus fasted for forty days after the Spirit led Him into the desert in preparation for a new season (Matthew 4:1–11; Mark 1:9–13). Immediately after He returned from His extended fast, He was launched into His ministry and called His disciples to partner with Him. Longer fasts have proven significant for many leaders in propelling them and their ministries into a greater destiny.

Different Types of Fasts

There are many different types of fasts out there. While some fasts are done for health reasons, to detox, or for cleansing, we will keep our focus specifically on biblical fasting connected to Christian spirituality for the purpose of growing in our relationship to God. The following are some of the spiritual fasts mentioned throughout Scripture:

- Absolute fast (also known as the Esther fast): no food or water (usually only three days, sometimes done in emergencies: Esther 4:16; Acts 9:9; Deut. 9:9, 18; Exod. 34:28)

- Full fast: water only fast (Matt. 4:2)

- Partial fast (also known as abstinence or the Daniel fast): restriction of diet but not completely abstaining from food (Dan. 1:15; 10:3)

- Private fasts: the most common of fasts, should be done undercover (Matt. 6:16)

- Regular fasts: done once or twice each week as a discipline (Zech. 8:19; Luke 18:12)
- Public/corporate fasts: sometimes called in times of group or national emergencies (Joel 2:15; 2 Chron. 20:1–4; Ezra 8:21–23)
- The Fire Fast: any of the spiritual fasts above done with the primary focus of intimacy, consecration, and revival (John 5:35)

Beyond the list above, you can also fast for a time from things like television, social media, shopping, sugar, sweets, coffee, alcohol, etc., which are likewise good practices. I did a social media fast one whole summer that helped clear my mind to write my book *Walking on Water: Experience a Life of Miracles, Courageous Faith and Union with God*. You can also fast from speaking like I did while working on this manuscript during a silent retreat at a monastery. There is also a fasting of time to come away with the Lord exclusively for a season.

Some people have medical conditions that prohibit them from certain kinds of food fasts, so these alternatives are great for those who still want to participate. It is important to realize that God can use anything to stir up hunger. While alternative fasts are good, the greatest desperation, spiritual hunger, and impact I have experienced have come while I was on a food fast.

Below, Heidi Baker shares about one unique fast God called her to right before the global pandemic of 2020 broke out. She had no idea why she was being invited to cancel everything, but God knew the whole time!

Fasting Time
by Heidi Baker

In 2019, the Lord wooed me and called me to cancel my schedule to spend forty days with Him in the desert in Israel. As I share this now, I am nearly crying just thinking about this because God knew what was coming in 2020 and He was preparing me.

He first showed me that He wanted to woo me away while I was deep in worship in Brazil at a massive meeting. I was face down on the carpet, lost in worship. Then everybody left but a little baby named Grace who prayed for me for forty-five minutes.

The Lord wooed me in that time and said, "Heidi, will you come with Me into the desert?"

My brain started to kick in, thinking, *Well, how long is that going to be?* and *Is that another forty-day fast? What are You asking of me?*

He said, "I am not commanding you, but I am wooing you into the desert. Will you come?"

I just lost it and started weeping. I said, "Yes, Lord. Whatever it costs, I will come."

I thought for sure that He would tell me to fast, but instead He said, "I am calling you to feast with Me in the desert."

Then I said, "How, Lord? And when?" I told Him how I was leading a ministry in thirty-some nations, living in Mozambique, and traveling around the world and that I had a very full schedule. All of these details started going around in my head.

Then He said, "I am wooing you in, will you come?"

At that moment, before I knew what it would mean, how much it would cost me, where it would be, how long it would be, or what we would be doing there, with everything that is in me, I said, "Yes, Lord, I will follow You anywhere."

I had so many meetings on my calendar in Mozambique and in other parts of the world during that time. But He said, "I want forty days in the desert. I want you to come and worship and feast on Me. I want this time." There was no way I could do it in the natural, but I was determined to obey the Lord to give Him forty days in Israel. I was determined to completely fast that time and give it totally over to Him. I put a big eraser through my schedule over those forty days. I obeyed Him to fast my schedule to feast on Him in the desert. This was in 2019 just before the world went into lockdown. Having just gone through 2020, I now realize how prophetic and powerful this time away was.

During that time, I got so deep in the Word of God. He showed me things to come. He showed me extraordinary hunger. He showed me more conflicts and war situations. He showed me so much about 2020 and gave me strength in that time. It was a time of fasting but also a time of feasting. I was so full of Him. I pushed away all the meetings and everything else.

One crazy thing that happened during my fasting to feast upon God in the desert season was that the defense for our Iris University was due to happen at that same time. This was the meeting that would give us permission to officially become a university. It was something I had prepared over ten years for, and it was planned to happen right in the middle of my wooed-away season with the Lord. I nearly broke my fast to hop on a plane back to Mozambique to be there for the defense, thinking, *I'll just go over there and defend the university, in Maputo, and then just fly back and finish the forty days in the desert.*

And the Lord said, "Is that what I asked of you?"

Birthing Iris University was one of my biggest dreams and one of my greatest challenges. It was a big "baby." I was pregnant for over ten years with this dream! But I said, "No, Lord, I will obey You. I will stay here."

I remember fasting from food all that day. I climbed up into the desert mountains by myself and worshiped at the top of my lungs. I wept as my team was there in Maputo to defend the university without me. I was obeying the Lord by not participating in seeing the dream He had given me so many years before come to fruition. It wasn't even like it was my idea in the first place; it was His.

After I came down the mountain back to where I was going to stay, I called my team. They told me that the defense never happened because some of the government officials in the education department did not show up. And there I was in the desert with the Lord, just worshiping, fasting, and adoring Him. He knew all along. I cried. I was so grateful that I obeyed God in that moment.

Later on in 2020, after three tries, the real defense happened and I was there! I was prepared in the Spirit. I was prepared in prayer. I was prepared in the depth and anointing that the Lord put on us for this dream fulfilled. In 2020, we passed that defense and got approved to officially launch Iris University.

Fasting is a beautiful thing. It actually has a lot to do with obedience.

Do you love Him more than your schedule? Do you love Him more than being connected with people? More than food? More than comfort? It's not that we're never going to have those beautiful blessings. It's just that He knows why, and He knows how He wants to call you to fast. When He is leading, fasting actually becomes a delight. This is what I am discovering for myself. Fasting time, when I don't meet with anybody and I just meet with Him, has been some of the most powerful and precious fasting ever.

CHAPTER 5

Motivations for Fasting

*The carelessness we have in our lives can
be dealt with only by experiencing the
fiery presence of God and allowing that
to be the motivating factor in our lives.*[1]

—A. W. TOZER

In different seasons, there can be different motivations for going on a fast. It's always best when we respond to the invitation and the leading of the Holy Spirit no matter what that might look like. There are also times when we simply want to love God by presenting Him with that sacrifice. As long as our hearts remain pure and our intentions are to honor God in the process, each one of these reasons for fasting is good and biblical. Here are a few examples of some of the reasons one might fast.

- Grow in hunger for God
- Regain focus
- Reposition or seek alignment
- Freedom from addiction or from habitual patterns of sin/bondage
- Help set others free (Isa. 58:6; Luke 9:1–2)
- Spiritual warfare (casting out demons: Matt. 17:21)
- Guidance in decisions (Dan. 9:2–22)
- As an act of humility (Ps. 69:10; John 4:8)
- Be refined
- Develop fruit of the Spirit, self-control
- Grow in intercessory prayer
- Sow into future seasons
- Set yourself aside as an act of consecration to God (Daniel)
- Prepare for stepping into greater measures of empowerment and anointing

It is also important to keep fasting in balance and not to come under the law, judgment, self-righteousness, or condemnation. Only the Holy Spirit can really sustain us on a fast, and we should always be led by the Spirit into all things. It is not by our own might or power but by His Spirit that we will be sustained during a time of fasting (Zechariah 4:6). For longer fasts, make sure God is on it, or else you may just be fasting and getting hungry. Other times, you may feel that you want to initiate a fast because you want to honor God, consecrate yourself, call out for mercy, sow into future seasons, or do it simply as an act of worship unto God. As long as your heart remains pure and you are not doing it to try and manipulate God or for personal and self-righteous gain, there are great rewards in fasting (Matthew 6:16–18).

Fasting to Bring Breakthrough

Many times, breakthrough can and does come through fasting (Matthew 17:21). While fasting is one key to bring breakthrough, it is important to realize it is not always the only key God calls us to use in a situation. There are times when breakthrough doesn't necessarily come through fasting alone, but instead by also loosing the chains of injustice, giving to the poor, or stepping out in radical generosity. In Isaiah 58, what was needed for breakthrough was setting the oppressed free paired with fasting. Other times, the key to breakthrough was found in giving away all of one's money to the poor (Matthew 19:21) or washing in the river seven times (2 Kings 5). Sometimes it came when friends tore off the roof of a house so one person could be healed (Luke 5:17–26), and other times it came simply by touching the hem of His garment (Matthew 9:20–22).

While the keys to our breakthroughs are different at different times, ultimately obedience is the greatest key. Sometimes what brought us a breakthrough in one season will not work in the next. That is why it is important to spend time with God and be led by the Spirit in all things. We are in a relationship with the Person Jesus, and it is important to respond to His leading. *Our healing and breakthroughs are not found in spiritual exercises but in a Person.* This is why it is important *not* to be led by spiritual disciplines but *to be led* by the Spirit.

With that said, fasting is one available key that Jesus regularly modeled and taught that can bring breakthrough in different areas, especially in the area of freeing people from demonic oppression. Many times, prayer with fasting is needed to overcome some of the more challenging spiritual battles we may face.[2] Further, if one can take dominion over his or her body with self-control through fasting, that person will also be able to take dominion over spiritual strongholds.

Why I Fast

For over twenty-five years now, I have integrated fasting into my lifestyle and have experimented with most of the fasts mentioned earlier at one time or another in my spiritual journey. I took a class called Spiritual Disciplines in my final year at Vanguard University where my professor, Bill Dogterom, had us all fast one day every week throughout the term. Though that was one of my hardest semesters, because I embraced the spiritual disciplines including fasting, I ended up getting the best grades that term. I have continued that rhythm of regularly fasting on Mondays ever since then.

So yes, I am one of those weird people who actually likes the spiritual discipline of fasting. It's not that I don't enjoy food; it's just that I love that I can do something to position myself to increase my hunger for God and accelerate my spiritual growth. I love that I can experience more of God simply by setting myself totally apart to hunger after Him. He is my portion and my prize.

I have experienced such radical focus, clarity in decision-making, and alignment with His perfect will when I have embraced fasting. Similar to putting on goggles under water, fasting has helped me see more clearly in the Spirit time and time again. I am by no means an expert—just someone who has discovered the joys of fasting and the increased intimacy and revelation that accompany it. I simply want to make sure everyone knows how special and easily accessible this truly is.

I Fast

- To encounter more of God
- To commune with God
- To grow in my hunger for God
- To be purified afresh for His purposes in my life
- To be set apart for Him

- To sow into the next season of my life
- Because Jesus fasted
- To tap into the wells of other revivalists
- To be ready to step into what God is doing
- To see breakthrough
- To refine my focus
- To seek wisdom and get clarity in my decisions
- To be aligned in His purposes for my life
- As an act of consecration and worship unto Him
- To stay full of the oil of the Holy Spirit

Fasting to Stay Full of the Oil of Intimacy

While the reasons I fast at different times vary, I generally and regularly fast the most because I want to stay full of the oil of His presence. I want to steward the fire of loving Jesus well. For certain types of lamps, oil is necessary to keep the fire burning inside. Fasting is one way of keeping our lamps full of oil so that the fire of God within us never goes out. If oil can also represent the Holy Spirit, another way of saying this is that fasting helps us to remain full of the Holy Spirit so that we can continue to burn bright for Jesus and be ready in season and out.

In Matthew 25:1–13, Jesus says that the kingdom of heaven is like ten virgins who took their lamps to meet the bridegroom. The only problem was that five of these virgins did not bring enough oil with them for their lamps. The other five brought extra jars of oil so that they would be ready at any hour to continue on with the bridegroom whenever he decided to show up.

The bridegroom hadn't yet arrived, and it was getting late. They all got tired and fell asleep. Then right in the middle of the night, they heard the cry that the bridegroom had arrived. They immediately awoke and trimmed their lamps so that they could enter in with the bridegroom. The five foolish virgins ran out of oil and were unable to continue the journey. They didn't have enough oil to keep their fire burning. They asked the five wise virgins for some of the oil they had stewarded for that very moment but were met with a clear "no."

The five wise virgins were not going to risk letting anything hold them back from this moment. The five unprepared virgins ran off in the opposite direction to get oil while the five wise virgins went straight into the wedding banquet with the bridegroom. Then the door to the party was shut.

By the time the foolish virgins made it to the front door, it was too late. Because of their lack of stewarding the oil, the bridegroom didn't even recognize these other virgins when they finally arrived. He said he didn't even know them. Jesus ends this story with a line I rephrase to go something like this: "Therefore, keep watch, remain full, stay ready, for we do not know when God is going to act next, appear in His glory, or demonstrate His power." God wants us to be ready so that even if it's midnight or an hour we least expect, we are full of Him and ready to step into all that He has for us.

I want my lamp to be so full of the oil of the Holy Spirit that *when* it's time to enter into the secret chambers with the One I love, I am ready. I want to be so full of the Holy Spirit that when it's time to cast out demons, love the brokenhearted, stop for the one in front of me, or step out in courageous faith, I will be ready to respond. I want to be flooded with God's love so much that the overflow spills out to those around me. I want to be like one of the five wise virgins who remained ready for the arrival of the bridegroom and were able to enter into all that God had for them. I want to be totally possessed by the Holy Spirit and always ready to step into the fullness of my God-given destiny. I want to be ready to advance the kingdom of God in season and out. Fasting is one of the ways we can be intentional about being filled with the oil of His presence and focusing our attention upon the Bridegroom.

Notes

1. A. W. Tozer, *The Fire of God's Presence*, 175.
2. Richard Foster, *Celebration of Discipline*, 60.

CHAPTER 6

The Bridegroom Fast
by Lou Engle

Jesus gave a key to His disciples to always live closely to the heart of Jesus the Bridegroom. That master key to the door of Jesus' burning affections was regular and extended fasting. Let me share a Scripture to help you understand. In the context of new wineskins, it says in Matthew 9:14–17:

> Then John's disciples came and asked him, "How is it that we and the Pharisees fast often, but your disciples do not fast?"
> Jesus answered, "How can the guests of the bridegroom mourn while he is with them? The time will come when the bridegroom will be taken from them; then they will fast.

> *"No one sews a patch of unshrunk cloth on an old garment, for the patch will pull away from the garment, making the tear worse. Neither do people pour new wine into old wineskins. If they do, the skins will burst; the wine will run out and the wineskins will be ruined. No, they pour new wine into new wineskins, and both are preserved."*

Here we see the followers of John the Baptist fasting often. These desert prophets were mentored by the Bridegroom's friend who spent most of his life fasting in the wilderness. When the Bridegroom Jesus came onto the scene, His disciples were not fasting at all but rather feasting. When questioned why, Jesus told John's disciples that the guests of the Bridegroom don't need to fast when the Bridegroom is present, but when He is taken away from them, then they will fast. He basically was saying, "The intimacy that My disciples are experiencing in this present moment is in their firsthand contact with Me. They are walking in My immediate presence and hearing My voice all of the time. So they are feasting now, not fasting. But when I leave them, they will fast; they will mourn for Me." Maybe better terminology for *mourn* would be *long for.* "When I am away, they will *long for* My presence. They will *fast* for My return." *Mourn* or *long for* in this context is synonymous with the word *fast*.

Why else did Jesus communicate this? Because when Jesus would leave them, they would have to know Him not according to the flesh but by the Spirit. They would need a new wineskin into which the new wine of the Spirit could be poured. Jesus was saying that through fasting they would more readily experience in the spirit that same presence of Jesus as when He walked with them in the flesh. The old wineskin of knowing Jesus in the flesh and feasting in His human presence would be replaced by a new wineskin dispensation of knowing Jesus in the person of the Holy Spirit. This knowing would be enhanced by fasting. Brothers and sisters, we live in the dispensation, the new wineskin, of the Bridegroom Fast.

Fasting brings you near to the central glory. Charles Spurgeon, the great preacher in England, once said, "Our days of corporate fasting were high days, indeed. Never were we closer to the central glory." This is what fasting is. The fleshly lusts, crucified in the fires of fasting, are subjected to the lordship of the Spirit and through fasting the soul feasts on the superior pleasures of heaven. Our heart affections are pulled upward to the central glory. Even though we can now, through the blood of Christ, step right into the presence of God, fasting is the divine door opener to deeper experiential encounters with Jesus. We can walk as close to Jesus as did His disciples—yes, even closer, for Jesus said in John 16:7, "It's better that I go away, for if I do not go away, the Helper will not come to you; but if I depart, I will send him to you." Isn't that beautiful?

Everybody thinks that John the Baptist was the most intense fasting man, and he was! In Matthew 3:4, it says that he ate locust and honey as his main diet. Our Daniel fasts are like feasts compared to his fasts of locust and honey. But then, it also says he fasted often. He broke his locust and honey main meals to eat nothing. John the Baptist basically lived his whole life fasting. He was a fasting prophet who prepared the way for the Lord. He was the friend of the Bridegroom.

However, I sensed the Lord speak to me one day and say, "The Bridegroom Fast of the last-days church will become more intense than the fasting of John the Baptist. The church is going to long for His presence more than even John because *she is the bride*; she will be more ravished by the love of the Bridegroom than even the friends of the Bridegroom."

Jesus said, "When I, the Bridegroom, am taken away from you, then My bride is going to fast." The closer we come to revival and His second coming, there will be intensified fasting. The Bride through fasting is going to bring the fulfillment of the end-times calling where it says she will be without spot or wrinkle. She will know experientially that she is completely loved. She will enter into the wedding feast of the Lamb (Ephesians 5:27). I believe that the wedding feast of the Lamb will not be about having all kinds of luscious foods at the table. I think we will eat there, but we won't need to because we will have the bread from heaven. We are going to be feasting on the very presence of the Lord, and fasting in this age will be the appetizer.

Entrance into His Presence

If you are just starting on your fasting journey, know that fasting is a God-given entrance into the continual presence of God, keeping the wineskin of your heart soft. It is why the bride will be without spot or wrinkle because she is going to live close to the presence of God.

The first time I fasted, it ignited a fire within me I had never previously known. It was a call from God. It truly was a call to fasting for fire, for burning desire. Inward fire comes through fasting. Jesus said of the fasting man, John, "He was a burning and shining lamp." Oh, that Jesus would engrave on the memorial stone of this generation, "They were a burning and shining lamp!"

I quit seminary in my twenties because I was looking for Acts 2 and couldn't find it there. Three of us made a vow we would seek Acts 2 no matter what it cost us. In those days, the Jesus movement was in full swing. Because of my vow, I moved to Maryland because there was a move of God going on there. Two thousand young people would get together every Tuesday to seek the Lord. The blind were healed, and miracles happened before our eyes; it was like returning to first love.

When I first moved to Maryland, I mowed lawns for five years. That was my seminary. I would pray in tongues behind that fifty-two-inch lawn mower, and no one could hear me. This was my school of prayer. Then someone told me about fasting. I will never forget what happened to me when I first started fasting. I was on the third day of a fast, and literally, as I was mowing lawns, I felt the presence of God so tangibly. I felt like angels were all around me. I felt the intimate fire of the Holy Spirit. I was so happy. I became so alive in God. Once I was so caught up in the revelation of who I was in Christ I began to declare, "It is not I who mow lawns, but Christ who mows lawns in me." I was living in a beautiful world.

From that point on, I fell in love with Jesus through fasting. I didn't realize at the time that that first experience was actually an entrance point to the calling on my life. For forty years since, I've given myself to fasting and mobilizing fasting and prayer for people to renew their first love.

I later read a book by Derek Prince called *Shaping History Through Prayer and Fasting,* which was about how the futures of nations, families, and lives are shaped through fasting. From that point on, I started doing longer fasts and haven't stopped since. Little did I realize at the time that God would later allow me to call the globe to fasting and prayer, even for forty-day fasts.

I believe that there is a measure of grace on my life for fasting. To be totally honest with you, I actually hate fasting because I love food. People think I am a great faster. However, I am miserable at it unless the Holy Spirit motivates me within. Without that motivation, I break my fast at breakfast. But when that motivation happens, I get excited because I know that something is about to change.

Fasting is a tipping point of moving into a new dimension of love for God and of making history with Him. Even though I dislike fasting, at the same time, I also love fasting. I have a love-hate relationship with fasting because, in fasting, I actually feast on God. This is really what happens. I deny myself the legitimate pleasures of food for the supreme pleasures of knowing God and of encountering Him. Fasting in His grace has literally always put the fire back in my heart.

If you want to return to the first fires of your life, you need to do what God says in Joel 2:12:

> *"Even now," declares the Lord,*
> *"return to me with all your heart,*
> *with fasting and weeping and mourning."*

Whenever I need to return to the Lord to get my heart tender again, I always return to fasting.

If you want to recover first love, learn to fast for the fire.

CHAPTER 7

God's Chosen Fast
by Randy Clark

I began my fasting journey in 1971 when I went on several one-to-three-day fasts for the purpose of praying for more anointing in my preaching before revival meetings. I noticed that many more people got saved in these meetings and that the anointing upon my life increased. I continued to grow in fasting during the years that followed and saw God move in unique ways. In the summer of 1984, I went on a twenty-day fast to pray for direction in whether I should leave the Baptist denomination. The very next day after I finished my fast, there was a petition to have me fired from my role as a pastor in the denomination, something I had peace about because God had prepared me while I was on the fast.

Then in 1985, I ventured on my first forty-day fast with the purpose of praying for more anointing for healing. Within hours after I ended this fast, I prayed for several people and saw a new anointing released to impart the office and ministry of healing to others. I've also gone on fasts simply to grow closer in my relationship with God. I remember one time in 1993 when I was so hungry for more of God that I was not going to eat until He touched me. It was fourteen days into the fast that He marked my life.

Before going to Toronto for the first time, I went on a fast to prepare and pray for increased anointing. God met me in a powerful way. Since then, I have fasted for increased healings, miracles, salvations, wisdom, and revelation. Fasting has been a big part of my walk with God and ministry.

The gift of fasting is not just for me, but it is freely available to us all to step into even more of what God has prepared for us. When God prepares to visit His church in revival, He leads them into prayer and fasting. But this is not just what He does on the national scale; it is what He also does in local churches, in families, and in individuals' lives.

Fasting most often occurred in the Old Testament during times of crisis and was often connected with times of repentance and seeking God. In the New Testament, Jesus talked about "when" we fast, not "if" we fast. In

Acts, fasting is seen as an act of seeking God's presence for guidance and for anointing for the task before sending out missionaries and setting elders in place. It is strongly connected to humbling ourselves before God and looking to Him for help in our time of weakness, lack of direction, natural and spiritual warfare, and desire for spiritual breakthrough or revival.

God leads us into deserts to seek Him and then brings us out of our deserts full of the Spirit. Jesus serves as a model in this. Jesus, Moses, and Elijah did extended fasts of forty days, and some famous people in church history have followed their example. I do believe that such extended fasts need to be led of the Lord to experience the grace for the fast to be able to sustain it for forty days. The Bible reveals fasts of various durations, and we must be sensitive to hear for ourselves what God leads us to do and when to fast.

Fasting in the wrong spirit or without humility, without seeking righteousness and justice, is seen in a negative light in the Old Testament. Fasting to be seen, as the hypocritical Pharisees and Sadducees did, was also spoken of negatively by Jesus. Fasting from legalistic motives to gain God's favor by our work would be against the spirit of Paul's letter to the Galatians.

My heart is that a new generation of Christians, laypeople, and leaders would discover the closet of prayer and fasting. We need to realize that fasting doesn't earn us "brownie points" or gain us "special favor." It also doesn't somehow make God indebted to us for our sacrifice. We must fast as an expression of our desire to know Him better, to change our lifestyle to focus on His presence. During a season of fasting, we can trust in the work of Christ alone for all ability to come boldly to the throne of grace in our time of need.

Fasting is a sign of our inability to effect the change needed in our society apart from His grace. It is a message from our earthly lives to heaven's throne that as we humble ourselves before Him, He alone can bring the increase in our lives. Let us humble ourselves in prayer and fasting that He might exalt Himself through us in due time.

I pray that you will trust God for a spiritual breakthrough for yourself, your church, your family, and our nation. May God in His sovereign grace move us by His Spirit to humble ourselves, seek His face, and turn from our wicked ways in order that He might hear from heaven, forgive our sins, and heal our land (2 Chronicles 7:14). May the world see our allegiance to our King Jesus and His kingdom and church above all other allegiances, parties, and race. May revival bring about, as it has in the past generations, a sense of the urgency for social justice. And may our fasting always include the understanding of the fast of Isaiah:

Is not this the kind of fasting I have chosen:
to loose the chains of injustice
and untie the cords of the yoke,
to set the oppressed free
and break every yoke?
Is it not to share your food with the hungry
and to provide the poor wanderer with shelter—
when you see the naked, to clothe them,
and not to turn away from your own flesh and
blood?
Then your light will break forth like the dawn,
and your healing will quickly appear;
then your righteousness will go before you,
and the glory of the Lord will be your rear guard.
Then you will call, and the Lord will answer;
you will cry for help, and he will say: Here am I.
If you do away with the yoke of oppression,
with the pointing finger and malicious talk,
and if you spend yourselves in behalf of the
hungry
and satisfy the needs of the oppressed,
then your light will rise in the darkness,
and your night will become like the noonday.
The Lord will guide you always;
he will satisfy your needs in a sun-scorched land

and will strengthen your frame.
You will be like a well-watered garden,
like a spring whose waters never fail.
Your people will rebuild the ancient ruins
and will raise up the age-old foundations;
you will be called Repairer of Broken Walls,
Restorer of Streets with Dwellings (Isaiah
58:6–12).

CHAPTER 8

To Obey Is Better Than Sacrifice

To obey is better than sacrifice
I want hearts of fire
Not your prayers of ice.

—KEITH GREEN

I recently read the story in First Samuel 15 of how King Saul, out of a desire to worship God, actually disobeyed Him. In the midst of a war where he had been commanded by God to utterly destroy His enemies, including all of the animals, Saul decided to spare the best sheep and cattle so he could give these as an offering to God. Though Saul's motivation was to give God a sacrifice, to do so in this instance was disobedience to His command.

God became angry with Saul because of his disobedience and sent the prophet Samuel to rebuke him. Samuel was heartbroken over what the king had done and cried out to God when he heard what had happened. Saul had broken a covenant with God by doing his own thing his own way, even making excuses. With the heart of God, Samuel confronted Saul and called him out.

> *Does the Lord delight in*
> *burnt offerings and sacrifices*
> *as much as in obeying the Lord?*
> *To obey is better than sacrifice,*
> *and to heed is better than the fat of rams.*
> *For rebellion is like the sin of divination,*
> *and arrogance like the evil of idolatry.*
> *Because you have rejected the word of the Lord,*
> *he has rejected you as king* (1 Samuel 15:22–23).

Even though Saul had good intentions in offering God a sacrifice of worship, he had not fully obeyed Him. God would rather have had Saul's total obedience than his sacrificial worship. Saul's choice cost him.

I wonder how many times, like Saul, I have chosen to offer God a sacrifice rather than fully obey Him. I mean, I can sacrifice eating food all day long, but if I never respond to the leading of the Holy Spirit in those times of fasting, I've missed it. And let me tell you, I've missed it more than once on my days of fasting. My heart grieves over my obsession with holiness and attempts to please God with my sacrifices for Him at the expense of obeying His still small voice to love the one in front of me.

More than our sacrifices, God wants our hearts fully devoted to Him.[1] He is way more concerned about our hearts being surrendered to Him than He is with us fulfilling religious practices.[2] David said in Psalm 51:16–17:

> *For the source of your pleasure is not in my performance or the sacrifices I might offer you. The fountain of your pleasure is found in the sacrifice of my shattered heart before you* (TPT).

The sacrifice of fasting serves the purpose of helping us yield our hearts more fully to Him. If our fasting doesn't lead us to have a more tender heart, respond more swiftly to the leading of the Holy Spirit, move with compassion, love the lost, give to the poor and needy, then we are not doing it right.

Hearts of Fire

There is a song by one of my favorite prophet singers, Keith Green, entitled "To Obey Is Better Than Sacrifice." It goes like this:

> *To obey is better than sacrifice*
> *I don't need your money*

I want your life
And I hear you say that I'm coming back soon
But you act like I'll never return…
To obey is better than sacrifice
I want more than Sundays
and Wednesday nights…
To obey is better than sacrifice
I want hearts of fire
Not your prayers of ice.

Even though this song was released in 1978, it still encourages and challenges me today. God wants "hearts of fire"—vibrant, beating, fleshly hearts—not "prayers of ice" riddled with our own agendas, offense, fear, bitterness, lack of action. Our sacrifice in fasting and devotion to God needs to be manifested in having hearts of fire.

Obsession

As I have continued on this journey in fasting over the years, I have realized that so many of the times I was "sacrificing" for the Lord, I also was shutting myself in and setting myself apart from the world. I had become all too comfortable being intimate with God in the secret place, but I became so afraid to shine Him in the open space. I had become numb, and I had to repent of living a dualistic lifestyle.

One morning as I was worshiping in my secret place time to the Lord, most likely while on a fast, God stirred my heart. I began to add some new lyrics to the Delirious song "Obsession." The following lyrics flowed out after I sang the chorus:

> *And my heart burns for You*
> *Not just in the secret place*
> *But in the open space*
> *Let my heart yearn for You*
> *Let my life, let it burn for You*
> *Today*

There was this awakening happening within me to not only be hidden away in the secret place but to *also* let my light shine in the open space. I had become so good at the spiritual disciplines, fasting, and spending time with God but was withholding His love from the world.

Matthew 10:8 says, "Freely you have received; freely give." We have all freely received from God so that we can freely give from that place of overflow. What He pours into our lives in the secret place is not just for our own consumption or to make us feel good. It should affect those around us and release His kingdom of love and power wherever we go.

I am realizing even now in my spiritual journey with the Lord that if I fast throughout my entire life but don't have love that flows from that sacrifice, it's worth nothing.

Love

The apostle Paul once said:

> *If I speak in the tongues of men or of angels, but do not have love, I am only a resounding gong or a clanging cymbal. If I have the gift of prophecy and can fathom all mysteries and all knowledge, and if I have a faith that can move mountains, but do not have love, I am nothing. If I give all I possess to the poor and give over my body to hardship that I may boast, but do not have love, I gain nothing* (1 Corinthians 13:1–4).

Love has to be the fruit of our increased hunger in fasting to know God more. The fruit of fasting for fire with the right motives will be a pure and contrite heart that loves others well, not self-righteous elitism that elevates itself above others because of the religious sacrifices made. Our fasting, worship, and devotion to God have to go beyond just a spiritual discipline. They must always result in obedience and a greater fiery love for those Jesus loves.

The Cost
by Heidi Baker

I remember one time I was in Singapore at a stadium meeting when the Lord wooed me away to fast and pray. At this event, the host told me I was scheduled to attend a big banquet. Singaporeans know how to feast and throw incredible banquets, so I knew this was going to be extravagant. Then the Lord spoke to me very clearly and said, "I'm asking you to come away with Me. I'm asking you to fast and pray and come away with Me."

I told my host, "I'm so sorry. I can't come to the feast, to the banquet. I have to be alone with the Lord."

As I was worshiping the Lord alone in my hotel during that time, God filled my room with His presence; it was powerful in there. Then suddenly I felt like taking a look at the schedule. As I opened up this very nice brochure for a well-organized stadium event, I saw that the banquet that was to happen right then was to honor *me*. Can you imagine? It was prepared in *my* honor with senior pastors from all over Asia, and it was printed in this beautiful brochure for all to see. Somehow I had overlooked this detail earlier on.

Right then I heard the Lord say to me, "Would you have changed your mind if you had known? Would you have disobeyed Me if you had known this before?"

I said, "Lord, I am so sorry." And I remember just breaking there, weeping on the floor.

That night as I got up to share the Gospel, I told the people that it was not my desire to offend any of them. In the natural, not showing up to a big banquet prepared with leaders from all over Asia to honor me would be like a huge slap in the face. It's just unbelievable. It's not like not showing up to a dinner party with friends; it's a whole other level. I was weeping for them.

As I shared with them that the Lord had called me to come away with Him during that time, the Lord said to me, "I want you to host a tea for them." He meant a real tea, a Singaporean tea, which is a very fancy tea. And I was going to have to cater this from my hotel.

Then I said to the whole stadium, "I want to honor you all. I want to invite all of the senior leaders and pastors to tea tomorrow at four. I don't know how it's going to happen, but I am inviting you." I remember this because it was going to be so expensive. Of course, I didn't have the money for this kind of thing. I had to ask my host to help me figure out a way to cater this, but I told them that I was going to pay for it.

They tried to convince me to let them pay for it, but I insisted that I would pay for it. I was the one who missed the banquet they prepared to honor me because I was with the Lord.

Then we had the tea, and it was so beautiful, and it was a lot of money. Then either just before or during the tea, someone handed me an envelope. They said, "The Lord just laid it on my heart to give you this offering." If I am not mistaken, it was around $2,300—the exact price of the tea! I just lost it, completely undone by the Lord. I remember weeping and hearing the Lord say, "Thank you for obeying Me."

Can you imagine what a lesson that was for the pastors to witness this unfold before their eyes? That was a life-changing event for me.

To obey is better than sacrifice. God is so worthy. He's the One in charge. He is the One I love. He is the One I serve. And He is the One for whom I want to be a laid-down lover at His feet. Whatever would bring Him pleasure, that is what I want with my little life. I feel God has led me to be a laid-down lover and to pay whatever the price.

Obedience

If we offer sacrifices to the Lord yet live unresponsive to His voice, we are religious robots living from rituals rather than relationship. However, if we set ourselves aside by fasting as an act of devotion to God and walk in obedience, there is a radical synergy and momentum that takes place that can set the world aflame.

Notes

1. In Mark 12:33, we see that love is more important than "all burnt offerings and sacrifices." And in First John 5:3, we see that those who love God obey His commands.
2. See Isaiah 1:11–20; 58:3–5; Jeremiah 7:21–23; Hosea 6:6.

CHAPTER 9

Practical Tips

God wants to flow through you with measureless power of divine utterance and grace till your whole body is a flame of fire. God intends each soul in Pentecost to be a live wire. Not a monument, but a movement. So many people have been baptized with the Holy Ghost; there was a movement but they have become monuments and you cannot move them. God wake us up out of sleep lest we should become indifferent to the glorious truth and the breath of the almighty power of God.[1]

—SMITH WIGGLESWORTH

Be Led by the Spirit

As we begin to dive into some practical tips in fasting, this is just a reminder to make sure you are being led by the

Spirit every step of the way as you venture out in faith. There are seasons for fasting and there are even seasons for feasting. We learned before that while Jesus was physically present with His disciples, it was a time for feasting, but there would come a time when the "bridegroom will be taken from them, and on that day they will fast" (Mark 2:18–20). It is important to be led by the Spirit always and to know what season you are in.

Also, be wise and seek counsel or medical advice first in regard to fasting if you have health issues. If you are pregnant, do not fast food but instead fast social media or something similar. For those who still want to participate in a fast but cannot because of health or weight issues, seek the Holy Spirit on how to be led in an alternative fast like those mentioned earlier.

Start Small

When beginning your journey in fasting, start small and celebrate your successes. If you have never fasted before, I would suggest starting with a smaller fast and skip two meals one day while drinking lots of water. If that is too hard, try drinking juice or a thicker liquid. For longer fasts, it is advisable to eat fruit just before.

Remember that fasting is not just abstaining from food; it is also filling your soul with something better: the fullness of the Holy Spirit. Spend the time you would normally have spent eating instead in worship, silence, prayer, meditating on God, reading the Word, praying with a friend, or waiting upon Him. If you have a chance, go to an isolated place where you connect well with God; for me, that is in nature. During your normal day, when you get hunger pains, turn your attention and affection toward God.

Uncomfortable

I find that days one and two are the hardest of any fast, no matter how long the fast is. This is when your body is detoxing. Usually after making it past day three, it gets much easier. During longer fasts, I notice my energy levels drop and I get cold. I also notice I am tired and need to take naps. I tend to wake up early or sometimes in the middle of the night.

Another thing to take into consideration is that many times one of the harder parts of fasting is not being as social since most events surround food. These events are still fine to join; however, doing group meals with people can sometimes get awkward when you are the only one not eating. I notice that I'm a bit more introverted than normal during fasts, and that's okay.

Richard Foster says that "more than any other Discipline, fasting reveals the things that control us."[2] During a fast, be aware of what comes up for you and take time to journal and process it. Are you easily irritated, feeling out of control, or experiencing some other extreme mood shift? What things are you running to rather than food? What themes are emerging in your heart? What relationships are being brought to the surface, and is He asking you to respond in a certain way? Is there anyone you need to forgive or be reconciled with? Is there anyone you need to reach out to or become more aligned with?

Ask the Holy Spirit what is really going on during these times and what He might be bringing up within you to heal. Ask God to go to the root of any issues that emerge. I encourage you to press in, worship, pray, scream, dance, run, intercede, beat a drum, contend, or whatever you feel you need to do to respond to God when the hunger gets severe.

There have been times when I have gone days without eating and at the same time have avoided God by staying busy. I filled up my schedule to mask the hunger pains rather than turning to Him in those times. I missed out on golden opportunities to dive in deeper with the King of kings. There have been other times when I have chosen to feast upon God's presence during a fast and have been surprised by rich encounters in His presence. Songs have been birthed, Scripture has been revealed at new depths, and healing has come as I positioned myself at His feet instead of trying to stay busy to avoid the hunger. Fasting is not just going without food; it must also be feasting on God.

The fast is the most effective when it is intricately woven together with communion with God.

While sometimes during a fast I experience increased connection to the Holy Spirit, have more prophetic dreams, and revelations of clarity, many times during a fast, I also don't feel a thing. Sometimes I'm just really hungry, weak, and even irritable. Other times, I am tired and weary from the lack of food while attempting to muster my strength to praise Him.

The amazing thing I have discovered though is that there has been a consistent pattern of God moving in a profound way in the days, weeks, or months following my fasts, even if I didn't feel anything in the process. While this was not the motivation for my fasts, most of my major breakthroughs and increased anointings have come in the season directly following a fast. Several of my books including *Silver to Gold*, *Water to Wine*, and *Life on Wings* were birthed after longer fasts. Destiny House ministry and Writing in the Glory were also both birthed following a long fast.

Pay Attention

Pay attention to the details and themes in what is being highlighted to you during a fast. Many times, we can hear the still small voice of God more clearly and see things we haven't been able to see before. Also, be aware of possible new alignments God may bring to you. Who is God high-lighting to you during this time? Who is reaching out to you during a fast? Are there potential divine connec-tions or anointed alliances He is bringing? Is He putting a burden on your heart for a specific person or nation? Is He putting a new idea in your heart? Is He redirecting your steps?

Don't be surprised if God changes your plans or redi-rects you during a fast. This is actually very common. In the process of focusing on His face and His agenda more precisely, many times people hear things from God that seem "out of the blue." These are from God and can be expected during a fast. Respond to the leading of the Spirit. What you hear from God, especially during a fast, may be your new assignment from heaven.

Don't get discouraged if you don't feel anything or see what you have been praying for during the fast. Setting yourself aside to feast upon Him alone is an act of wor-ship, which He is pleased about whether you experience a tangible immediate result or not. Furthermore, while you are setting yourself apart and consecrating yourself to the Lord, He is at work behind the scenes on your behalf even if the timeline is different than what you imagine. From the first day Daniel set himself aside to pray, God heard his prayer and dispatched an angel to help him (see Daniel 10:12–14). And remember, ultimately at the core, you are fasting to feast upon God and grow closer to Him more than anything. This alone is a priceless investment.

Learning to Thirst

I once did an Esther fast in conjunction with a call Lou Engle put out, and this was the hardest fast I have ever done bar none. Even though it was only three days, it was going completely without food and water. I remember feeling so incredibly weak. I dreamed of having just one sip of water.

What was different about this fast from all others was that it was the first time I learned about *thirst*. I had become acquainted with understanding spiritual hunger, but when both food *and* water were removed, I learned something about spiritual thirst I had never accessed before. The story of the rich man asking the beggar Lazarus for just one drop of water in hades made sense to me in a new way (Luke 16:19–31). I experienced more of what the psalmist meant in Psalm 42, when he wrote that as the deer pants for the water, so his soul thirsts for God. I felt like I, too, could cry out to God along with David:

> *I thirst for you,*
> *my whole being longs for you,*
> *in a dry and parched land*
> *where there is no water* (Psalm 63:1).

There's Grace

It is really important to give yourself grace during a fast. If you end up breaking the fast prematurely or before the original goal you had set for yourself, don't beat yourself up or come under condemnation (Romans 8:1–4). Celebrate each small victory. If you have never fasted before and you were able to fast one meal rather than two starting off, celebrate that you are on your way. There have been times when I couldn't even make it to the end of my one-day fast and I had to eat. The grace had lifted for me to continue, and that's okay.

The beautiful thing about fasting with pure motives and the right perspective is that we are not fasting to try and prove a point to anyone or even to ourselves; we are simply positioning ourselves *to know God better*. We fast to encounter more of God. There are no rules here. We do it to fall more in love with God. The more we practice fasting, the easier it becomes.

How to Break a Fast

Practically speaking, it is important to break a fast well to avoid injuring your stomach or harming your body. Your body is the temple of the Holy Spirit, so make sure to be wise and steward what goes in there. Breaking a fast is usually good with liquids, fruit juices, and then moving on to fruit and vegetables. Slowly integrate more regular foods into your diet depending on how long the fast was. Generally, you can come off shorter fasts with a light meal of fruits or vegetables and then work your way toward weightier meals.

Coming off of a fast will vary for each person and will depend upon how long the fast was. For longer fasts, be gentle and slowly ease back into your regular diet so that you don't shock your system. It is important to replenish your body with the proper nutrients. Even if you make it to the end of a longer fast, the effects of going without food and the right nutrients may take some time to recover from.

I drink a lot of coconut water before, after, and sometimes even while on a liquid fast because it is rich in electrolytes. Taking vitamin supplements can also be useful. The main thing to be aware of on the other side of a fast is that your body has gone without nutrients and will need some time to replenish them to get back to normal. Do some research to learn the best way for you to come off of a fast, and record what works and what doesn't for future fasts.

Notes

1. Smith Wigglesworth, "The Substance of Things Hoped For," *The Pentecostal Evangel*, October 25, 1924, in *Smith Wigglesworth: The Complete Collection of His Life Teachings*, compiled by Roberts Liardon (New Kensington, PA: Whitaker House, 1996), 464–465.
2. Richard Foster, *Celebration of Discipline*, 55.

CHAPTER 10

Longer Fasts

Our call should be to be a burning bush.[1]
—A. W. TOZER

Forty-Day Fasts

I feel like I am very much still a novice in regard to forty-day fasts. To this day, I have yet to do a full forty-day fast with only water, although I have many friends who have done so and would be much more qualified to speak about it. The fasts I will refer to included liquids, which I felt peace from the Lord about. It is important to clarify that I had already begun to fast regularly, including several seven-day fasts, before I engaged in the longer ones.

The first forty-day fast I did on liquids was in 2003 while I was working at Starbucks. Following this time, I released two thousand copies of my small booklet called "From Silver to Gold" at Lou Engle's The Call in San Francisco long before I met him. This booklet was the beginnings of what would later be my first book, *Silver to Gold: A Journey of Young Revolutionaries,* which came to fruition in 2009 and became a core message for my life and ministry.

I did my second forty-day fast during the busy holiday time in November through December 2011. God showed me a day or two beforehand that I was to go on this forty-day fast. I knew He was preparing me for my ordination with Heidi Baker, which would be exactly forty days later from the time I started the fast. This fast was a way for me to take my ordination seriously, consecrate myself, and prepare to step into all that He had. The timing was also significant because I had recently finished my Ph.D. in England, moved back to Southern California, and was getting ready to move to Redding, California.

This fast was incredibly challenging because it was during the Thanksgiving and Christmas holidays. Yes, that's right—family gatherings around the dinner table, and I was the only one not eating turkey dinner!

On the first day of the fast, I began to work on a small testimony book called *Water to Wine: Experiencing God in the Canary Islands* with the intent to get it out within the forty days. On day five of my fast, while still in Orange

County, I went to a local library determined to work on that book when I faced spiritual warfare head-on.

As I was working on my manuscript in the library, a woman started staring me down and then literally began to hiss at me. I couldn't believe it! But because I was fasting, I had the courage to address the situation rather than come under it. As she was hissing at me, I looked her directly in the eyes and said, "Excuse me. I'm sorry—what did you say?" She didn't respond. I attempted to focus back on my work and did my best to ignore the evil being released in my direction.

As she continued to stare me down, I remember thinking, *This demon doesn't know who they are dealing with, especially during my forty-day fast!* And at the same time: *Oh no! Am I going to have to cast a demon out in a public library?*

Finally, this person got up and left, and I was able to continue with my writing along with the other person near me who could continue working in peace and quiet. If I hadn't been fasting, I would have likely gotten upset, frustrated, had my mind thrown off for the rest of the day, and I would have not confronted the situation. But because I was fasting, I was able to take dominion, hold my ground, and not come under the attack or give attention to the enemy. Fasting helped me to focus. I ended up releasing my book on the last day of the fast, forty days later, the same night I got ordained by Heidi Baker in Redding on December 31, 2011.

In the month that followed my forty-day fast and ordination with Heidi, while still without a job, car, or steady place to live, I had two significant prophetic dreams that later came true. It was also during this same time period that I went through one of the most intense, challenging, and humbling times in my entire life right before birthing Destiny House on my birthday, February 18, in 2012. The struggle was real, but that story is for another time. You can read about it in my book *Walking on Water*.

It was also in early February 2012, just a month after my fast, that I launched the first ever Writing in the Glory training with three others in a coffee shop. This has since become a workbook, a workshop, an ecourse, and I have gone around the world and catalyzed numerous revivalist authors to birth their first books. In March 2012, I also finished my book *Life on Wings: The Forgotten Life and Theology of Carrie Judd Montgomery (1858–1946)*.

This fast played a significant role in helping prepare me to step into a greater measure of my destiny in the months and years that followed. To this day, I am still riding on the momentum from what was birthed immediately following that longer fast. Its impact is still bearing fruit today, over a decade later. Now, that is a powerful investment!

My third forty-day fast a few years later was unique. Both this fast and the previous one came upon me suddenly. Once I felt God's stirring, I was moved by the Spirit to start my fast within one to two days following. This third forty-day fast was a preparation time to sow into a new season. This was easier than the previous one in some ways because it was during the summer season, and thankfully there were fewer social activities going on around me at that time. This fast was also unique for me in that I did something I had never done before on a previous fast.

Halfway through my fast on day twenty, I found myself at a wedding celebration. I was torn. I was with my friends and longing to partake in the celebration but was desperately hungry, tired, and losing stamina. There on my dinner table sat my bottle of mango juice. This was awkward. I was hungry. Jesus celebrated and turned water into wine at a wedding, so after an insightful conversation with a friend, I decided to do something crazy on this fast—*eat!* And eat whatever I wanted! There on day twenty, I decided to enjoy this wedding party and savor one of the most delicious meals of my life! After that meal, I continued back on my fast.

Toward the end of this most interesting fast, I started to lose a lot of the willpower to finish and ate a few select meals before the forty days ended. Eating a total of four meals out of 120 opportunities over the forty days is still a great investment, and I have no regrets. That is the wonderful thing about fasting—there are no laws or rules. There is no one to punish or judge you if you fulfill your desired fast or not. When fasting purely to grow closer in relationship, it's between you and God. It's not a goal to achieve or a religious duty to fulfill; it's all devotion and worship unto Him.

Though I didn't fully complete this fast like I had intended to, I believe God celebrated my efforts. And I believe that fasting a little bit, even if you don't complete the full fast, is a lot better than not fasting at all. There is always something to learn in the process. As we exercise and build up our fasting muscles, they will be strengthened over time.

Next, read about Heidi's unique experience on a forty-day fast. I love how it never looks the same for anyone. God uniquely meets each one of us differently, and that is a beautiful thing.

"I'm not a drug dealer. I promise!"
by Heidi Baker

I remember the first forty-day fast that I did. The Lord called me away and said, "I want to be alone with you." I was doing my Ph.D. in the U.K. at that time. I did a lot of twenty-one-day and seven-day fasts before this, but forty days are longer ones. And I'm not Lou Engle; I don't do a forty-day fast every eighty days! He probably is about to do another one at any time now. But fasting has truly marked my life.

I recently did two forty-day fasts. I remember that the hardest part of those fasts would be on the airplane when the airline workers would come with their food trays. During one of my forty-day fasts, I was still speaking all over the world and had to fly a lot during the fast. Every time the food would come while in the airplane, so many times I wished the Lord would just let me have something to eat.

And then the stewardesses would say, "Why aren't you eating? Please eat. You need to eat something." This could have been a seventeen-hour flight.

I'd say, "No, thank you," again and again, every time they brought along a tray. I remember my flesh screaming, "You look like a kook. These people think that you are kooky."

Then I remembered a friend of mine telling me that drug dealers don't eat in planes because they swallow the drugs. Airline workers are always cautioned when people don't eat, and they pin these types of people as possible drug dealers. So finally I realized what was going on. It wasn't because I wasn't eating that they kept urging me to eat, but they literally thought I might be carrying drugs. I didn't even realize this until later. It was a challenge. But I had to come to terms with answering the following question from God: "What will you care about: the opinions of man or what I've asked of you?"

The cost sometimes is very much about pushing aside human opinion. Even in the church, people say, "That's awesome that you are fasting," or, "Good for you." But there are also people who will be angry with you. Other people might think that you are crazy. In the world, when they see a person not eating for days, they can be really confused.

I remember my mother weeping once and thinking I was crazy and in a cult. She thought I was going to die if I didn't eat something. I had to keep on loving my mother while staying firm to what the Lord had asked of me. There is a cost, but He is worthy of it all.

The interesting thing is, in the forty days or the twenty-one days and all fasts, God tends to meet me the most before I start, when He calls me to it. He crashes in on me and meets me in that place at the invitation. He undoes me and gives me strength to obey through the whole fast. Then He tends to touch me again afterward. I don't know why that is. I've heard other people say that when they are fasting, they have nightly dreams and visions. For me, I am just hungry a lot of the time. But I spend a lot of time reading the Word of God, and I get absolutely undone when the fast is over.

I remember going to Portugal for the first time toward the end of one of my fasts. I walked up to the top of a mountain to end my fast with communion there. That is when God just crashed in on me. At the end of my forty-day fast there on that mountain, He said, "Thank you for obeying Me. Thank you for listening to Me." It was unbelievable just how He broke in at the beginning and at the end of the long fast so strongly.

Note

1. A. W. Tozer, *The Fire of God's Presence*, 74. He says, "We are not called to be great. We are not called to be beautiful. It may be beautiful in the fire, but not in your boldness or courage. Our call should be to be a burning bush."

CHAPTER 11

Corporate Fasts

*The fire on the altar must be kept burning; it must
not go out. Every morning the priest is to add
firewood and arrange the burnt offering on the fire
and burn the fat of the fellowship offerings on it.*

—LEVITICUS 6:12

Corporate and regular fasts can be powerful. John
Wesley had a rhythm of fasting two different days
each week with his friends and encouraged those in his
movement to follow his example. William J. Seymour was
on a ten-day fast with some friends when the Azusa Street
Revival was birthed. Corporate fasts are dynamic because
they bring in an element of accountability, encouragement, and mobilization for greater breakthrough. Many
times, corporate fasts, coupled with prayer or worship,

bring a powerful focus, synergy, and acceleration in the things of God.

Community Rhythms

I consistently invite others to join me in my regular weekly fast. The Destiny House community that I led from 2012 to 2019 fasted together every Monday. After Sunday dinner, we would skip breakfast and lunch the next day. Then on Monday evenings, we would break our fast together with a family meal. We tried to live in the refining fire of God and remain full of the oil of the Spirit. When something came up that needed a miracle or breakthrough, we were already fasting so we could link arms in prayer. When missionaries or leaders came to visit, we were able to fast and pray ahead of time to partner with the breakthrough they were seeking.

Each summer, we also did a one-week fast to pray into the upcoming year together. That same week of fasting, we also hosted open worship encounter times together each day. This time of sowing into the upcoming season had a powerful impact on the whole year following, where we hosted worship encounter times every Friday morning and literally saw God do miracles before our eyes.

Now that I am leading School of Revival with people from around the globe, we also have adopted fasting one day a week. This helps us live refined and consecrated unto the Lord. Embracing a rhythm of regular fasting together also helps prepare us so that when it's time to step out in faith or even step into longer fasts as we are led of the Spirit, we are ready. Fasting consistently helps build these spiritual muscles.

When we adopt a rhythm of fasting and practice it in the peaceful times, we will be ready when a spiritual battle arises. Navy Seals train and prepare rigorously so that when it's time to be sent on a mission, they are ready. They don't get ready right before they are sent. They live ready. That is our mandate in the spiritual sense, and fasting can help us prepare in a similar way.

Fasting and Ministry

Three days of fasting and prayer were set apart at the Mission for more power in the meetings. The Lord answered and souls were slain all about the altar the second night. We have felt an increase of power every night.[1]

—Azusa Street Mission (May 1907)

I regularly try to set apart some time to fast before ministering at an event or conference. I have seen in my own life and ministry that so much more gets released when I set myself apart to fast and pray before an assignment. Fasting helps me get God's heart for His people, refines my focus in the prophetic, and helps me be more in tune to flow with the Spirit. Fasting helps me steward and sow into the opportunity God has entrusted me with. I have also seen the power of God move in profound and increased measures when my team and I fast together leading into an event.

If I have the opportunity, I also encourage others to set aside at least one day to pray and fast before attending a meeting where I will be ministering. This increases both their hunger and expectation as well as positions them to receive all that God has for them. Most of the time, my prayer is that God will lead them into encounters and defining moments through the revival history testimonies I release.

I remember one time a few ladies in Destiny House and I fasted several days leading up to a speaking engagement I had at Bethel School of the Supernatural in 2015, where I was planning to release the testimony of the Welsh Revival. I remember the preparation beforehand felt so heavy, like we were carrying something significant that needed to be released. It felt like we were pregnant with something weighty.

After our preparation in prayer and fasting, we stepped into that session, and the power of God crashed in like I had never previously experienced in my personal time of ministry. People were screaming, getting set free, being marked by the fire of God. Some were even laid out on the floor groaning as if they were giving birth to something in the spirit. From what I heard even years later from some of the students who were there that day, God marked them with fire and impregnated them with seeds of destiny. The fire of God fell in a powerful way. Fasting was a birth pang in the process before the labor was complete.

Later on that year and the next, God opened up doors for me to also share about the Azusa Street Revival with the school. This was to prepare them for the Azusa Now event Lou Engle was putting together later that school year. Once again, I have no words that can describe what was released during those sessions. Releasing these powerful testimonies from revival history paired with fasting, intercession, and inviting the angelic was explosive. God just showed up, and I tried my best to get out of His way. A student who was at a couple of these Azusa sessions will give you a better idea of what God released.

Commissioned as a Revivalist Under the Power of God

by Mathieu Bernard from Switzerland,
Bethel School of Supernatural Ministry graduate

It all started in November 2015. I was sitting in class at Bethel School of Supernatural Ministry. Jennifer came at the end of the day just to pray for the Azusa revival. I have never had any manifestation of the Spirit. The Holy Spirit was spoken of in my church back home, but I don't feel that we were actually connected to Him. I've never been drunk in the Spirit or had any other manifestations that we commonly see today. Being in this environment, I was curious for myself to experience this.

But something changed when Jennifer hit the stage that day. I began to experience something that I've never felt with any other speaker. What impressed me was how she spoke for only five minutes. When she did, she said, "Let's acknowledge the presence of God in here." At that moment, the presence of the Holy Spirit came so strongly that half of the students were touched and each one showed visible signs of God touching them.

All of a sudden, something passed through my right arm, and into my chest, and then my throat. The feeling was like freezing cold water. Suddenly, I felt a freedom like I've never felt before. A freedom to worship God in a new way. I started to worship in thankfulness, praying with all my heart to God concerning Azusa. The presence of God began to grow thick around me, and I found myself hanging on to the bar next to my seat.

Fast-forward to March 2016. Jennifer came back to our school. As soon as I recognized her, I said to my wife, "It's Jennifer. There is something special about her because God touches my life every time she comes." As soon as I finished my sentence, something came behind me like the feeling of a gust of wind. It touched my head and went all the way down to my feet. I asked the woman next to me if she felt anything, and she had. Then another wave hit and then another and another. For the first time, I understood what people meant when they said God hits you like a wave.

I understood in that moment that God wanted to do something in me that day, so I surrendered, lifting my hands and my eyes toward heaven as He touched my heart. A few moments passed, and suddenly I began to cry uncontrollably as new waves of God began to touch me once more. I opened my eyes to see Jennifer on stage sharing history about Evan Roberts. As I saw the picture of Evan, I began to shake.

Jennifer continued, "Do you know how Evan started revival? By praying for salvations."

I began to laugh and cry hysterically. I was shocked, because only a couple of months before this, I was sitting at my kitchen table reading about Evan Roberts. As I read about this revivalist, I began to weep. I was so moved in my spirit that I started praying for fifty salvations to come in my own country.

I knew in that moment, as I found myself weeping again in school just from hearing about Evan, that God was doing something in me that I couldn't explain. During this time, I had never heard the audible voice of God, but in that moment, God touched me so deeply and said to me, "I'm giving you the mantle of Evan Roberts." Overwhelmed with His peace, I was sealed in the presence of God. God Himself commissioned me as a revivalist, and I knew from that day forward I would never be the same.

God chose Jennifer to deliver not only a key word to my heart—but to the very thing I was called to do. The mantle that God created me to carry was handed to me that day, and I am forever grateful.

Fasting and Pioneering Revival

All who were present came to the altar and made a full consecration and prayed for a baptism of the Holy Ghost and of fire, and that night it came. Fifteen came to the altar screaming for mercy. Men and women fell and lay like dead. I had never seen anything like this. I felt it was the work of God, but did not know how to explain it, or what to say.[2]

—Maria Woodworth-Etter

Fasting is a key for pioneering revival. When you feel like God is wanting to birth something new through your life, go on a fast. I remember going on a ten-day fast in August 2019 while in Norway in preparation for my

European Revival tour that would follow. I had just facilitated the first ever Writing in the Glory workshop in Norway and then had spoken at a church on how to not miss revival. The next day, I decided to go on a fast in preparation for launching the first ever live School of Revival in Switzerland, Czech Republic, and then Belgium.

On day four of the fast, I did a revival night on the Azusa Street Revival in the basement of a church in Oslo that Pentecostal pioneer T. B. Barratt had planted. God moved in a special way. On day five of the fast, I had a day to myself where I poured out my heart to God. He delivered me from the stronghold of a lie that had impacted me up to that point.

I ended my ten-day fast in Switzerland and the very next day, on August 30, 2019, launched the first ever School of Revival with some of the Destiny House family joining me. After I released the testimonies of the Welsh Revival and the Azusa Street Revival, the fire of God fell powerfully during the sessions. One of the students named Matthew got marked by God at the school. He said:

> I felt this gush of wind, like someone was walking behind my back. I literally felt my t-shirt move and started to have goose bumps all over me. At that point, I heard people break down in the room, pouring out before the Lord. I knew He was there in that moment.

I encountered God in a new, crazy way. I've always wanted to experience and to see His glory, and this was a life-changing moment for me.

Following my time in Switzerland, I continued on to do a School of Revival in both the Czech Republic and Belgium before finishing my trip off in France with a few revival meetings. Less than a year later, and after being redirected to return to Orange County in late 2019, I stepped out by faith to host the first School of Revival online in May 2020. This was during the early days of the COVID-19 pandemic and lockdown and was only supposed to be a one-time thing. God breathed on this so much that it has continued through the entire school year and is still running up until the time of writing this book.

Many times, right before we are about to pioneer something new or step into a radical breakthrough, God prepares and refines us by stirring us to fast so we can partner with birthing His heart. I had no idea when I went on that ten-day fast while in Norway in 2019 that I was sowing into something that would later become a movement known as School of Revival, impacting many around the world.

Notes

1. "At Azusa Mission," *The Apostolic Faith* 1:8 (May 1907), 2.

2. Maria Woodworth-Etter, *Acts of the Holy Ghost; or The Life, Work, and Experience of Mrs. M.B. Woodworth-Etter, Evangelist* (Dallas, TX: John F. Worley Printing Co., 1912), 42–43.

CHAPTER 12

Breakthroughs in Fasting

by Lou Engle

Rewards for Fasting

There are breakthroughs that are not readily available in normal prayer that are available in fasting. In his book *Shaping History Through Prayer and Fasting,* Derek Prince drew a triangle with a line segmenting the top part of the triangle.[1] Beneath that line are answers we get to ordinary prayer. On the top of that line, however, is where there are mega-breakthroughs only available through fasting and prayer. There is a dimension of fasting that drives us to a place of desperation where we get ahold of God in ways we wouldn't otherwise.

Too many people have dismissed fasting and say, "Well, I don't have to do that." And I respond by saying,

"Well, do you have to pray? Do you have to give to the poor or give tithes and offerings? Absolutely." Fasting is part of the tripod of discipleship. Jesus says, "*When* you fast, *when* you give alms, and *when* you pray." He doesn't say "if." He also communicates that if we are His disciples, then we will fast. He says, "*When* you fast, go into your closet, a secret place, and don't blast it all over the place (unless it is a corporate fast, that is, which I've called a lot of, and which I've broken a lot of). And when you fast, the Father in heaven will see when you are fasting in secret and He will *reward* you in public" (see Matthew 6:1–18).

There is a reward to fasting. And I believe that reward most importantly is intimate encounter with the Lord.

Fasting and the Demonic

After my personal breakthrough with fasting while mowing lawns, I went on another fast with a friend where we prayed for ten days for the anointing to cast out demons. On the tenth day of my fast, my pastor called me and said, "Lou, there is a young woman here who needs prayer." I went over and joined my pastor. As she began to pray and forgive her brother, demons started to manifest and speak through her. She began banging her head on the table. When we prayed for her "in the name of Jesus," she almost immediately received deliverance. I was stunned. On the tenth day of fasting came the breakthrough.

Another time while on a fast, I was co-leading a home group of about twenty people. A guy walked in without even introducing himself or saying hello. We had no idea who he was; he just sat down. When everyone was dismissed for the night, he stayed around afterward.

When I asked him what he wanted, he asked, "Could you cast out my demons?"

And I was thinking, *Oh no!*

So my friend and I took him to a back room where I interviewed him to find out what was going on. I remember thinking, *I don't know about this.* We had fasted ten days in preparation to see God move in a greater way. Jesus says in Matthew 17:21, "This kind does not go out except by prayer and fasting" (NKJV).

So I did a token prayer and said, "Lord, if there are any demons in this guy, drive them out in Jesus' name."

Immediately the guy started flopping like a fish. Literally, for two hours, he flopped over the couch and continued flopping and manifesting.

Finally, we got a breakthrough and he stopped flopping. Then he looked at me, smiled, and said, "Thank you very much," and walked right out the door.

Corporate Breakthroughs in Fasting

Another time later on, ten or fifteen of us went on a thirty-day fast. We gathered together every night to pray for prophetic worship to explode in such a way that people would be saved during the worship times in our church. Every evening during the fast, we prayed specifically for people to get saved in the midst of worship. The night before the thirtieth day of the fast, I was reading First Samuel 10 where the sons of prophets were playing their musical instruments and King Saul, under the influence of their worship, prophesied all day long.

As I was reading that passage, I began groaning and entered into what the Spirit prays for us with groans too deep for words (see Romans 8:26). The fasting had prepared me for this birthing process. *Fasting is the womb to give birth to new eras, new days, and new movements of God's activity in our lives.* As I groaned, I knew that something was going to happen the following day, Sunday, during the worship time.

I was actually the worship leader, believe it or not. I have an old gruff voice, but I can sing! As I began to spontaneously sing a song, a lady came down from the balcony and took the microphone next to me. That should never have happened, but God was orchestrating the divine symphony. When I started singing, "We gaze upon Your purity..." she started to sing the echo: "We gaze upon Your purity..."

I continued on, "We gaze upon Your beauty. We gaze upon Your loveliness; holy incense do we bring," and she continued to sing the echoes. Then when I sang, "And we gaze into an open heaven…" All of heaven broke out into that place! It was like pandemonium. People started screaming, shouting, dancing. No one could stop. Then there was shouting: "We see angels!" No one could preach. People started getting saved, and for weeks following, many others would also give their lives to Christ in the worship service. It was a miracle. Through this radical manifestation of His presence, the Lord showed me the power of corporate prayer and fasting.

Through a series of breakthroughs in my life in relation to fasting, God has shown me a pattern, a trajectory. It started with myself when I experienced personal breakthrough in fasting. Then I saw breakthrough in individuals who needed deliverance. Then I saw it corporately in our church after thirty days of fasting for breakthrough. Then I saw it in our city in a revival that was poured out in 1994— an outpouring of the Holy Spirit that went for three years. The Lord was showing me, "I am giving you breakthroughs through fasting in ever-increasing spheres." Little did I know that He would call me to call hundreds of thousands worldwide in fasting. He was creating faith in my heart for worldwide breakthrough every step of the way.

Note

1. Lou is referencing the book by Derek Prince called *Shaping History Through Prayer and Fasting* (New Kensington, PA: Whitaker House, 1973, 2002).

CHAPTER 13

Dreams and Revelation

by Lou Engle

D id you know that in fasting, you make your life a landing strip for revelation? In almost every extended fast I've done, dreams and prophetic whirlwinds have come. These dreams have encouraged me and often revealed and birthed my next prophetic seasons of life and the divine assignments God has called me into.

In fasting, we get understanding from heaven. In Daniel 10:2–3, it says:

> *At that time I, Daniel, mourned for three weeks. I ate no choice food; no meat or wine touched my lips; and I used no lotions at all until the three weeks were over.*

From the first day Daniel set his face to seek under-standing, an archangel came in swift flight to give him revelation. After twenty-one days, the angel said to Daniel:

> *Do not be afraid, Daniel. Since the first day that you set your mind to gain understanding and to humble yourself before your God, your words were heard, and I have come in response to them. But the prince of the Persian kingdom resisted me twenty-one days. Then Michael, one of the chief princes, came to help me, because I was detained there with the king of Persia* (Daniel 10:12–13).

From the first day Daniel set his face to seek the Lord with fasting, *war was inaugurated in the heavens.* In response to Daniel's posture of seeking revelation from heaven, an archangel was immediately dispatched to deliver the mes-sage. The demonic prince of Persia withstood him for twenty-one days until Michael the angel prince over Israel came to his support and together they gained supremacy and remained there victorious on the field of battle over the kings of Persia; this is simply astounding. Daniel, in fasting and prayer, presided over a governmental shift of an entire empire. "O Daniel, greatly beloved."

"What is man? You've crowned him with glory and honor and put all things under his feet" (see Psalm 8).

Did you know that when we are moved to fast in the timings of God and in a spirit of deep humility, we too inaugurate war in the heavens?

People say, "Fasting doesn't change God; it changes you." In one sense, that's true. It does change you. It changes the wineskin of your soul. But in Daniel's case, he didn't need to be prepared. The archangel told Daniel that he was "highly esteemed" in heaven (Daniel 10:11). This is what heaven thinks about a friend of God who fasts and gives birth to *His* purposes. This is the supreme vocation: prophetic intercession.

If God could find one woman or one man like Daniel, what might happen in this world?

Daniel was crying out for revelation. In fasting, you actually begin to open your soul to receive revelation. That's why dreams come in fasting. Jesus says, "Ask, seek, and keep knocking" (see Matthew 7:7). Asking is normal prayer. Seeking is when you begin to really call on God desperately, and fasting is like knocking. When you keep knocking, you are saying, "I will not take 'no' for an answer." Jesus says in Luke 11:13, "How much more will your Father in heaven give the Holy Spirit to those who ask him!"

Bill Johnson says, "There is a storeroom of heaven filled with revelation for your life. The Spirit within us searches that storeroom, searches the deep things of God." Did you know that you have a built-in search engine inside of you?

Fasting in the Holy Spirit is that search engine. It is a God-ordained means to help you discover God's thoughts and ideas concerning your life hidden in the storage room in heaven. You begin to search for God, and He begins to give you dreams. Dreams then reveal and direct your future. Obviously, the Scriptures are God's foundation for judging prophetic revelation, but dreams are often so real and specific they shatter false thought systems and hurl us into divine adventures and destinies.

God Is Drawing You

Fasting is the greatest power for the shifting of history.

There is a new breed that's coming, a new generation that's going to go further than any other generation in fasting and prayer for the shifting of government, shifting of education, shifting into revival. Fasting is God's way of bringing forth these divine shiftings. I believe if you are reading this, you are also a part of this movement. Your heart might even be burning right now, and you may feel a drawing in your spirit to live this kind of life.

It is important to realize that when God puts an inward desire in your heart for fasting, it is not the devil tempting you. I can't fast a day if I have no inward motivation. I'm the worst. Once I said to my wife, "You know, honey, I'm going to fast today." She responded by saying, "What do you want for breakfast?"

Whenever the Lord begins to spur me inside to fast, I get excited because I know something new is about ready to break out or some mega-breakthrough is going to take place. When God ignites this fire inside of you, fasting becomes a joy, not a legalistic religious rule to check off. When you need a breakthrough and when nothing else works, I encourage you to go into fasting-and-prayer mode.

When you get that fire for fasting, don't put it off. In Psalm 27:8, David said it like this: "When You said, 'Seek My face,' my heart said to You, 'Your face, Lord, I will seek'" (NKJV). *Fasting is cultivating a habit of spiritual responsiveness to the inward movings of God.* He put that desire in you. Don't wait around and say, "Well, I'll do it down the road." Step into fasting when the fire is burning. When He says, "Seek My face with fasting," move in response to Him.

Moving in response to God's stirrings was an important key to David's life. Some people are on a twenty-year program of obedience, but David's was one of *immediate responsiveness* to the inward pull of the Holy Spirit. I call it my "Come away, My beloved" tug. When God begins to draw you, don't put Him off. Move toward Him with fasting and watch for the reward.

I'm living in the rewards of fasting that I did thirty years ago. Believe me, there will always be a reward because God keeps His promises.

CHAPTER 14

A Spirit of Burning

God's ministers are "a flame of fire." He
wants men and women all on fire. He wants
us not only saved from sin but on fire. The
Holy Ghost is dynamite and fire in your soul.[1]

—AZUSA STREET MISSION (May 1908)

When we walk with Jesus, our hearts will be ignited with His fire, and there will be a spirit of burning inside of us. We will be compelled to know Him more. Let me share a story with you to demonstrate this. On the same day Jesus was resurrected from the dead, He made a sneaky appearance to two of those who had been following Him and were heartbroken over His death just days before. As these two Jesus followers were leaving Jerusalem on the road to Emmaus, Jesus came up and walked beside them, but they were kept from recognizing Him.

When Jesus asked what they were discussing, they were shocked that He hadn't heard the news that their beloved Messiah had been crucified. More so, these two had heard the reports from the women at the tomb who saw angels and believed that Jesus was actually alive. Some of their friends even went there to see the empty tomb for themselves. After hearing this, Jesus began to expound the Scriptures that spoke about Him all the way from Moses to the prophets (see Luke 24:13–27). Then:

> As they approached the village to which they were going, Jesus continued on as if he were going farther. But they urged him strongly, "Stay with us, for it is nearly evening; the day is almost over." So he went in to stay with them.
>
> When he was at the table with them, he took bread, gave thanks, broke it and began to give it to them. Then their eyes were opened and they recognized him, and he disappeared from their sight. They asked each other, "Were not our hearts burning within us while he talked with us on the road and opened the Scriptures to us?" (Luke 24:28–32)

Following this, they immediately returned to Jerusalem and found the eleven disciples and the others gathered with them. They told them that the rumors were true; Jesus had been raised from the dead, and they were witnesses to that fact. While they were still speaking, Jesus suddenly appeared in their midst and surprised them all (see Luke 24:33–36).

Earlier when these two disciples had walked with Jesus on the road to Emmaus, there was a *burning* within their hearts. In a similar way, there is something about fasting that brings us into a place of radical communion with Jesus. Fasting ignites a *spirit of burning* inside of us.

Like those walking on the road to Emmaus, will we respond to the burning in our spirits as we walk with Jesus? Will we compel Him to stay with us and not pass us by? Will we urge Him to come into the home of our hearts, dine with us, and explore the deepest crevices of our hearts?

Let me tell you a little secret. If you want to become a burning one for Jesus, embrace a *lifestyle* of fasting. Fasting is an accelerator into His fiery presence and will help you focus on the face of Jesus always. When we gaze into His eyes that are "like blazing fire," we become transformed into burning ones for His glory (see Revelation 1:14).

Focus

But make Jesus, the Anointed One, your focus in life and ministry (2 Timothy 2:8 TPT).

Fasting helps us focus our attention on Jesus. The word focus comes from a Latin word that was once used to describe fire.[2] If one takes a magnifying glass to capture the sunlight in one focused ray, it can literally start a fire. If focus can be used to start a fire in the natural, can you imagine what kind of revival fires might be ignited when we similarly focus all of our attention on Jesus?

When a handful of burning ones at the turn of the twentieth century focused wholeheartedly on the One Thing, revival was ignited. One of my favorite quotes in relation to the Azusa Street Revival is from eyewitness Frank Bartleman. When describing some of the early Los Angeles prayer meetings that happened before the revival was birthed, he said:

> There was no closing at 9 o'clock sharp, as the preachers must do today in order to keep the people. We wanted God in those days. We did not have a thousand other things we wanted before Him.[3]

These hungry ones did not have "a thousand other things" they wanted before God. Wow! What incredible focus they had on the Lord in those early days. It's as if they felt within their veins something massive was on the horizon, and they knew they needed to throw aside all that hindered so that they could fully press in.

Then on April 9, 1906, when a handful of African Americans gathered together in a little house on Bonnie Brae Street with their only agenda to seek God for the all-consuming baptism of the Holy Spirit, He answered their cries. Many of these pioneering Pentecostals were on a ten-day fast and reading Acts 2 every day when the Holy Spirit crashed in and lit a flame that is still burning to this day.

Alongside a remnant of burning ones contending to receive more of the Holy Spirit, Jennie Evans Moore experienced a radical baptism of the Holy Spirit that night. She said:

> For years before this wonderful experience came to us, we as a family, were seeking to know the fulnes [sic] of God, and He was filling us with His presence until we could hardly contain the power... On April 9, 1906, I was praising the Lord from the depths of my heart at home, and when the evening came and we attended the meeting the power of God fell and I was baptized in the Holy Ghost and fire.[4]

It was as these focused lovers threw off "a thousand other things" so they could be consumed with God alone that revival fire was ignited. This fire quickly outgrew their home and later became known as the Azusa Street Revival. The Azusa fire catalyzed and significantly contributed to the spread of global Pentecostalism, which is still impacting us over a century later.[5]

What might a generation look like today that says "no" to a million things, to say "yes" to the One Thing? We have a lot more distractions vying for our attention and affection today than these early Pentecostals had a century before us. Today, the price is higher. The cost is greater. And because of this, I believe the fire will be even brighter.

Kairos

Many of those who gathered at the Bonnie Brae house were on a fast together when the revival was ignited. Fasting helps position us to step into all that God has for us, especially during unique *kairos* moments in time. *Kairos* is the Greek word in the New Testament for *time*. It is translated as "the right time," "a set or proper time, opportunity, due season, short time," or "a fixed and definite time, the time when things are brought to crisis, the decisive epoch waited for."[6]

On November 16, 1905, just months before the Azusa Street Revival exploded on the scene in a *kairos* moment in time, Frank Bartleman felt a stirring similar to what many of us might be feeling today. He said:

> The current of revival is sweeping by our door.
> Will we cast ourselves on its mighty bosom

and ride to glorious victory? A year of life at this time, with its wonderful possibilities for God, is worth a hundred years of ordinary life. "Pentecost" is knocking at our doors. The revival for our country is no longer a question. Slowly but surely the tide has been rising until in the very near future we believe for a deluge of salvation that will sweep all before it. Wales will not long stand alone in this glorious triumph for our Christ. The spirit of reviving is coming upon us, driven by the breath of God, the Holy Ghost. The clouds are gathering rapidly, big with a mighty rain, whose precipitation lingers but a little.

Heroes will arise from the dust of obscure and despised circumstances, whose names will be emblazoned on Heaven's eternal page of fame. The Spirit is brooding over our land again as at creation's dawn, and the fiat of God goes forth. "Let there be light." Brother, sister, if we all believed God can you realize what would happen? Many of us here are living for nothing else. A volume of believing prayer is ascending to the throne night and day. Los Angeles, Southern California, and the whole continent shall surely find itself ere long in the throes of a mighty revival, by the Spirit and power of God.[7]

Might we be feeling a similar stirring today? In this hour, do we, too, feel an all-consuming hunger to press into God because we can sense something imminent on the horizon? Are we currently in a *kairos* moment? Are we as a generation pregnant with the next Great Awakening or the next Azusa Street Revival?

What if this next revival will be greater than all of the other ones combined? What if we are riding on the momentum of all the previous revivals put together, a tsunami wave of revival so big that it will bring a convergence of the ages together? Will we choose to lean in and partner with what God is pouring out, or will we let it pass us by because it might look and feel different than what we expected? Or maybe, just maybe, the beginning of this massive tsunami wave of revival has *already* begun.

I believe you are reading this book right now because God is raising you up as a spiritual mother or father to help steward this incoming billion-soul harvest that has already been inaugurated. You are here because you have responded to the invitation to go all in.

Let me speak a hard truth to you right now. If you are not deeply rooted in Jesus when this next radical move of God is poured out in all its fullness, you will be swept away. Now is the time to be more firmly established in Him and positioned to ride this next wave so that it does not destroy you. Fasting will help you get more grounded in Him.

I truly believe we are living in a *kairos* moment of time. Heroes will begin to arise from the dust of obscure and despised circumstances. Those who have been hidden in the secret place will soon be unveiled to the world. For many reading this right now, that is you!

Burning one, there is no more time to waste. Now is the time to come off the sidelines and step into the front lines. You were born for such a time as this. You are destined to burn. Now is your time to arise, tend to the inward flame, and set this world ablaze with the fire of God.

Notes

1. *The Apostolic Faith* 2:13 (May 1908), 2. It continues on to say, "He wants us to have not only the thunder but the lightning. The Holy Ghost is lightning. He strikes men down with conviction, slays and makes alive."
2. To read a whole chapter on the theme of focus and its origins, see chapter 6 entitled "Focus" in Jennifer A. Miskov's *Walking on Water: Experiencing a Life of Miracles, Courageous Faith and Union with God* (Bloomington, MN: Chosen Books, 2017), 72–80.
3. Frank Bartleman, *How Pentecost Came to Los Angeles: As It Was in the Beginning* 2nd edition (Los Angeles, CA: Frank Bartleman, originally published in 1925), 102. This is now printed by Christian Classic Ethereal Library (Grand Rapids, MI) and accessible at http://www.ccel.org/ccel/bartleman/los.pdf.

4. Jennie Moore, "Music from Heaven," *The Apostolic Faith* 1:8 (May 1907), 3. To read the full version of her account, see Jennifer A. Miskov's *Ignite Azusa: Positioning for a New Jesus Revolution* (Redding, CA: Silver to Gold, 2016), 117–118.

5. Read Jennifer A. Miskov's *Ignite Azusa: Positioning for a New Jesus Revolution* (Redding, CA: Silver to Gold, 2016) to learn more about the Azusa Street Revival.

6. Strong's Concordance, https://www.blueletterbible.org/lang/lexicon/lexicon.cfm?Strongs=G2540&t=KJV. See Ephesians 5:15–16 for an example of the word *kairos*.

7. Frank Bartleman, *How Pentecost Came to Los Angeles*, 39.

CHAPTER 15

Tend to the Inward Fire
by Lou Engle

If you have an inward burn, yield to it. John the Baptist was a burning one because he was a fasting man. He cultivated that inward fire with fasting; his lifestyle was one of fasting for fire. Jesus wrote on the epitaph of John's life: "He was a burning and shining lamp and you enjoyed his light for a little while" (see John 5:35).

Yet what we have today are pseudo-prophets who think that they can speak on their mobile phones and be prophets when they have never paid the price to get a voice. What we hear is *noise, noise, noise*. What we need is *voice, voice, voice*. John said, "I am the voice of one crying in the wilderness" (John 1:23 KJV).

Why not shut up for a while and get a word that burns inside of you that you try to not say or put up on YouTube. It's not that you can't have a message on YouTube, but in actuality, are you touching true prophecy? A person can give a prophetic word that sounds so good but doesn't touch our hearts. Another person can give a word with bad delivery, but when it reaches our hearts, it has sticking power. It won't leave us. Why? Because the prophecy was forged by a voice from heaven; it was not forged by a good idea.

Jeremiah said, "I tried to shut the word in, but I got weary of shutting; it became like a fire within me, like a hammer, that shatters the rock" (see Jeremiah 20:9). Today we have too many noises out there and not enough voices. *Voices are forged in the deserts of fasting, not in the desserts of feasting.* Make sure you have a word from heaven before blasting it out there.

I also want to urge you not to be impatient to get a stage. God will forge your stage with years of fasting. There were twenty years of silence in my life when no one would let me preach because I had no character. For twenty years, I was silent. All I could do was preach in prayer to God. So I just lifted my voice and preached to God in prayer. Then one day, a woman came and said, "I am going to pay your salary because you are going to start something with fasting and prayer that will change the destiny of the nation."

And in one day, God said, "You've been faithful in your fasting, and with your little prayer meetings, so I'm going to pull the curtain and take your prayer meeting public."

When I walked onto the National Mall in Washington, D.C. in the year 2000 for The Call D.C., by 6:30 a.m. there were already 270,000 people there and by noon, 400,000.

They came to a voice, not a noise.

I don't understand why I was chosen. It is important not to despise the years of preparation in silence. Fasting does something inside of you. It breaks you. It's hard. But it's worth getting ahold of the Bridegroom.

The Nazirite Call

The taglines that helped mobilize 400,000 or more were, "Prophets are forged in the deserts of fasting, not in the dessert of feasting. We have taught our children to feast and play; the times demand that they fast and pray. This is not a festival; it is a fast."

The message we preached years prior to The Call D.C. was the message of the Nazirites who separated themselves from the legitimate pleasures of this world for the extreme pleasures of knowing God. They became the countercultural revolutionaries like John the Baptist, like Samuel, like Samson. They were raised up in the darkest days of a nation, and their radical consecration and their love for God were like a pendulum swinger. It was to call an apostate generation back to the Lord their God. And God called them the Nazirites. He said in Amos, "I have raised up from among your young men prophets and your sons Nazirites. But you commanded my prophets not to prophesy and your Nazirites to drink wine" (see Amos 2:11–12).

There will always be the temptation from parents, from religious people, from pastors saying, "You are too extreme. America is so far gone." But the Nazirite call is a calling to extremism—extreme love and extreme devotion. God rebukes those who sit there and try to keep young people from burning with an extreme passion. Yes, we all need wisdom and spiritual fathers and mothers in our lives, but God loves the fire of the young person and He'll never want to put it out. Always remember to stay humble under the mighty hand of God.

This Nazirite call was the message we preached back then. I remember my son at age thirteen saying, "Dad, I want to do a forty-day fast." He was barely even a teenager. He had just turned thirteen! I didn't know what to say to him. He said, "I don't want to cut my hair. I want to be a Nazirite to The Call." The Nazirites would not drink wine or eat certain types of sweets including grapes. It was a fasting lifestyle that God produced. The mighty pendulum-swinger prophets were the Nazirites. He said, "Dad, I don't want to play baseball for seven months before The Call. I just want to do a Daniel fast. And all

I want to do is pray with you for revival." I didn't know what to tell him.

At four in the morning the next day, I heard the audible voice of God three times. He said, "America is receiving her apostles, prophets, and evangelists, but she has not yet seen her Nazirites." I woke up and I knew that the Lord had said, "Let the young man burn. Let him go all out." He did a forty-day fast on juice and smoothies. He didn't play baseball. He did a type of Daniel fast; then after the fast, he continued on for seven months.

When he prayed in front of 400,000 young people, he said, "Let the long hairs arise. Bring up the Nazirites." I'll never forget when 400,000 people, mostly high school-ers, roared. When the video of his prayer was shown in the Philippines, the Spirit fell on a youth group that birthed the Jesus Revolution in the Philippines. One hundred fifty thousand people gathered in the Philippines, and then for five years, throughout the nation, it was fasting and prayer. Then into Vietnam, they were doing underground fast-ing and prayers. Then Thailand, Southeast Asia, up via the rim, and it went all over the world. My son, with that kind of consecration and fasting, shifted the world in seven months of his life.

I want to challenge you who are reading this—don't be afraid to go extreme. You won't hurt yourself. Do a three-day fast. Do it on water. You might feel really weak, and you might get headaches and nausea, but what is happening is that you are detoxing all of the poisons so you can have a brand-new wineskin. I also want to encourage you not to condemn yourself if you start fasting and you fail. I've failed a million times. God loves that you're actually desiring and stepping into it. He will honor your efforts every time. You can't fail in Him. He is proud of you for stepping out.

I remember the young people saying to me, "Whenever we hear you speak about the Nazirites, we feel our hearts burning inside." You might be feeling the same thing right now. You might want to be one of those burning ones I just described. You might want to be a sold-out lover of God, a bride whose fire is not just good religion or American Christianity religion but is the fire from heaven. That's the Nazirite burn. So, if you have that, watch over it with all diligence.

I know what it means to lose that fire. I have to recover it as soon as possible. You want to have the inward burn of God. To have that inward burn is the most desirable thing that you could ever have.

A high calling demands high separation and total consecration.

God is desiring for you to burn.

Chapter 16

The Fire Fast

I do not know of anything that America needs
more today than men and women on fire with
the fire of heaven; and I have yet to find a man
or a woman on fire with the Spirit of God that
is a failure. I believe it is utterly impossible.
They are never discouraged or disheartened.
They rise higher and higher and it grows better
and better all the while. My dear friends,
if you haven't this illumination, make up
your mind you are going to have it. Pray, "O
God, illuminate me with Thy Holy Spirit!"[1]

—DWIGHT L. MOODY

Have you noticed there is a difference between Christians and burning ones? Between those who settle for a one-way ticket to heaven and those who are all in, increasing in hunger and devotion, and are willing to pay any price to love God with everything inside of them?

My heart is that as you actively join me in this journey in fasting to know God more, you will be ignited with a burning inside of you so strong that it won't let you settle for mediocre Christianity. I want your life to be so marked by an all-consuming fire that it stirs you to catalyze others around you to love Jesus wholeheartedly. My desire is that you, too, will become a burning one who never burns out, shining brightly for all to see.

The Fire Fast

The bush became beautiful in the fire.[2]

—A.W. TOZER

I want to now introduce you to a specific type of fasting I like to call the Fire Fast. The Fire Fast is simply taking any of the spiritual fasts mentioned earlier (absolute, full, partial, regular, Daniel fast, etc.), and adding one specific emphasis to that fast—an all-consuming focus on Jesus. I integrate the Fire Fast into almost all of my spiritual fasting.

Embracing the Fire Fast is responding to an invitation to live in the fire so that our only attention is on Jesus. In the Fire Fast, we welcome a baptism of fire to destroy every other competitor vying for a place of prominence in our hearts. We give the Holy Spirit permission to remove all distractions so that we can run after Jesus wholeheartedly with reckless abandon. It's a fast with one specific goal: loving Jesus with our whole hearts, minds, souls, and bodies. It's a desperate call for the Lord to enflame us with His love. It is an unyielding devotion to Jesus that says, "No matter what it costs, I am running after You" (see Hebrews 12:1–2).

Once we see the fire in His eyes, all of our efforts will feel like the least we can do to position ourselves to behold His glory. When we are so in love with Him, fasting won't even seem like a sacrifice anymore (see Song of Songs 8:7 TPT).

In fasting for fire, we welcome the fire of God to reignite first love, to set us apart wholly for Him, and to release revival through our lives. While there can be many variations of the Fire Fast, the three that I want to introduce here are the Fire Fast of Intimacy, the Fire Fast of Consecration, and the Fire Fast of Revival.

The Fire Fast of Intimacy

You won't relent until You have it all
My heart is Yours
Come be the fire inside of me

Come be the flame upon my heart
Come be the fire inside of me
Until You and I are one

—MISTY EDWARDS

The first, and I believe the most important of all the Fire Fasts, is the Fire Fast of Intimacy. When the fire of intimacy is rekindled with the Lover of our souls, something beautiful is awakened within us. When we reconnect our hearts to His fiery presence, the fire within us is ignited once again.

Everything from our lives flows from the vibrant love relationship we have with Jesus. When we fast with a focus on reigniting the flame of our first love, the other effects of consecration and revival naturally follow. He is the Source of all fruitfulness, signs, wonders, miracle power, and revival flowing through our lives. We don't pursue intimacy with Him to get any of these things; we do so because we simply want more of Him. These fruits are many times byproducts that are naturally birthed from our union with Jesus.

The Fire Fast of Intimacy is responding to the invitation to shut out all distractions, silence all competing lovers, and focus our affection and attention on loving the One who gave His all for us. It's a set-apart time of worshiping Jesus with a heart posture of pure *adoration*. It's a time to sing and pray in tongues and lavish Him with overflowing love. It's a time to be still and listen to His stirrings to have all of us (Psalm 46:10). It's a time to slow down, take off all of our armor, be vulnerable, and let Him into every space in our hearts. It's a time to be uncovered and let Him cover us in His glory love. It's pure communion with the living God.

Solomon communicates the heart of this invitation from God to take us deeper. I encourage you to read this out loud and make it your prayer in this moment:

> *May your awakening breath blow upon my life*
> *until I am fully yours.*
> *Breathe upon me with your Spirit wind.*
> *Stir up the sweet spice of your life within me.*
> *Spare nothing as you make me your fruitful*
> *garden.*
> *Hold nothing back until I release your fragrance.*
> *Come walk with me as you walked with Adam*
> *in your paradise garden.*
> *Come taste the fruits of your life in me* (Song of
> Songs 4:16 TPT).

David also speaks into the fire of intimate love God wants to have with us:

> *My heart is on fire, boiling over with passion.*
> *Bubbling up within me are these beautiful lyrics*
> *as a lovely poem to be sung for the King.*

*Like a river bursting its banks, I'm overflowing
with words,*
spilling out into this sacred story...
*Now listen, daughter, pay attention, and forget
about your past.*
Put behind you every attachment to the familiar,
even those who once were close to you!
*For your royal Bridegroom is ravished by your
beautiful brightness.*
Bow in reverence before him, for he is your Lord!
(Psalm 45:1,10–11 TPT)

These verses speak of hearts being on fire with passion for the Lord.

The Fire Fast of Intimacy is about being absorbed in the heart of Jesus. It's about being obsessed with Him and Him alone. It's about going on a journey into deeper intimacy together. This fast is not about works or ministry or even revival; it's about being in love and expressing those feelings affectionately with the Lover of our souls. The Fire Fast of Intimacy is primarily focused on adoring the King of kings with no other agenda than to love Him well.

The Fire Fast of Consecration

All believers are called to a one hundred percent consecration. God has no two standards of consecration for the foreign missionary, and the home Christian. We cannot find it in the Bible. One is called to consecrate their all as well as the other, as God's steward, in their own place and calling.[3]

—FRANK BARTLEMAN

Consecration means to be set apart, sanctified, prepared, holy, purified, appointed, and dedicated to the service and worship of God. In Romans 12:1–2, Paul says:

Therefore, I urge you, brothers and sisters, in view of God's mercy, to offer your bodies as a living sacrifice, holy and pleasing to God—this is your true and proper worship. Do not conform to the pattern of this world, but be transformed by the renewing of your mind. Then you will be able to test and approve what God's will is—his good, pleasing and perfect will.

Living a consecrated life is becoming a living sacrifice unto the Lord. It is an act of worship. It is not something that happens to us but something that we choose to embrace *daily* as we freely surrender and offer our lives wholeheartedly to the Lord.[4]

The Fire Fast of Consecration is an intentional time to be set apart and refined by the fire of God. It is inviting God to come and search our hearts and remove anything that could hinder us from more of Him in our lives. In Matthew 3:11, John the Baptist says, "I baptize you with water for repentance. But after me comes one who is more powerful than I, whose sandals I am not worthy to carry. *He will baptize you with the Holy Spirit and fire."* This fast is where we intentionally pray for a fresh baptism of fire upon our lives.

Fasting itself can be likened to a refining fire. Rather than wait for sanctification to happen through trials and tribulations, we choose to place ourselves into the furnace of consecration so that we can be purified. Everything contrary to His nature gets exposed and burned up in the fire.

Many times, before we are able to see Him clearly and focus wholeheartedly on worshiping Him in spirit and in truth, we need to be refined in the fire to clear away all of the distractions. Embracing the Fire Fast of Consecration helps purify our hearts so that we can see Him more clearly. This is not something we can make happen, strive for, or do on our own, but we can position ourselves to welcome this refining fire to purify our hearts.

The Fire Fast of Consecration is a call to total abandonment and absolute surrender. During this fast, we intentionally welcome the fire of God to purify and bring alignment in every single area of our lives including our relationships, dreams, struggles, and more. We say, "Lord, send Your fire!" And when He burns things away, we say, "More fire!" This can sometimes be painful because God may strip away toxic relationships that are holding us back or may remove things in our lives that are keeping us bound. He may even ask us to release good things back to Him that we are no longer called to carry into this new season.

The Fire Fast of Consecration is only for the brave. To embark on this type of Fire Fast, you will need to have a firm foundation in your view of and relationship with the Father. You will need to know that He is for you and trust that He has your best interests in mind. As you posture your heart in surrender, He may take things away from you that you have clung tightly to. Many times, He does this so that He can give you something better in return, and usually that is more of Him. When you know and trust that God is for you and is only pruning you to make you more fruitful (see John 15), you will welcome this refining fire in your life and freely surrender all to Him. When you understand that He is only removing things from your life that are causing pain or holding you back from greater fruitfulness, you will embrace this fire.

This healthy process of letting go does not necessarily take away the pain that may come from this loss. Going through the fire can be painful, but it is necessary at times to refine and purify the gold inside of us. Waiting upon the Lord in silence is one sure way to welcome His refining fire to search our hearts. In the silence, there is nowhere to hide. When He is given that space, that's when He likes to come in deep to do heart surgery.

I regularly pray for a baptism of fire in my life. When He begins to expose things like pride, idolatry, offense rising up within me, or when relationships begin to break down, when disappointments come my way, when pain surfaces, I say to the Lord, "Send Your fire. More fire. Burn, burn away anything that is not pleasing to You."

When we learn to willingly step into and *live* in the fire, when the fire comes, it does not utterly destroy us because we have learned to live refined. However, if we run away from the fire of God's love, mercy, judgment, correction, and holiness, when the fire comes upon us because He is lovingly drawing us back to Him, it is much more painful and costly. It is so much better to embrace a *lifestyle* of living in the fire than waiting for God to refine us through it. Fasting is one of the ways to stay in the fire. And be encouraged:

> *When you walk through the fire, you will not be burned; the flames will not set you ablaze* (Isaiah 43:2).

Like Shadrach, Meshach, and Abednego, when you are led into the fire, Jesus will be with you and only the ropes that are binding you will be destroyed (see Daniel 3). And when you are ready to embrace this fire of consecration, the invitation is yours.

The Fire Fast of Revival

One evening, July 3, [1905] I felt strongly impressed to go to the little Peniel Hall in Pasadena to pray. There I found Brother Boehmer ahead of me. He had also been led of God to the hall. We prayed for a spirit of revival for Pasadena until the burden became well nigh unbearable. I cried out like a woman in birth-pangs. The Spirit was interceding through us. Finally the burden left us. After a little time of quiet waiting a great calm settled down upon us. Then suddenly, without premonition, the Lord Jesus himself revealed himself to us. He seemed to stand directly between us, so close we could have reached out our hand and touched him... A heaven of divine love filled and thrilled my soul. Burning fire went through me. In fact my whole being seemed to flow down before Him, like wax before the fire. I lost all consciousness of time or space, being conscious only of His wonderful presence. I worshipped at His feet.[4]

—FRANK BARTLEMAN

The third Fire Fast I want to highlight is the Fire Fast of Revival. This works best following the previous two Fire Fasts and many times comes as a natural result of these. It is important that the foundations of first love and a consecrated life are established before or in conjunction with pursuing revival so that we will be able to steward the fire of revival well. If revival breaks out and we are disconnected from relationship with Jesus (see Matthew 7:21–23) or are not walking in holiness and purity, the revival could actually destroy us. Holiness is an important container to steward revival.

The Fire Fast of Revival is important to give us God's heart for the people He loves. It moves us beyond an inward spiritual discipline and seeks to let that fire within spread out to others around us. The Fire Fast of Revival is seeing beyond ourselves. It is asking God to not only break our hearts for what breaks His, but it also includes a *response*. If we are never activated in the midst of all of our fasting and prayer, we are no better than the religious Pharisees. We must also be moved to action to become the hands and feet of Jesus on this earth. The Fire Fast of Revival helps us do just that from a place of already being deeply connected to the Source.

The Fire Fast of Revival is intentionally seeking God's heart for this world and partnering with heaven in prayer and fasting to see these things come to pass. It is being willing to go on assignment wherever the Lord leads. It's a listening and response fast. It's receiving God's burden to intercede for the lost and also being responsive when He leads us to action.

In this fast, as in any fast, it is important to realize that through your intercession, God may be calling you to be that answer to your own prayers. One time Rees Howells was interceding for a missionary family in Africa who needed a replacement. During the prayer meeting, God revealed that it was he who was supposed to be the answer to his own prayer. Be ready to both pray God's heart and also to become His heart in action.

The Fire Fast of Revival is all about calling for God to pour out His Spirit in unprecedented measures over our own lives and also over our families, friends, cities, regions, nations, and the world. It is where we begin to intercede to see God's kingdom come. It is where we make ourselves available, just in case we are to be the answer God wants to send. It is positioning ourselves to respond like Isaiah did when he heard the voice of the Lord saying:

> *"Whom shall I send? And who will go for us?"*
> *And I said, "Here am I. Send me!"* (Isaiah 6:8)

Notes

1. D. L. Moody, *Short Talks* (Colportage Library) in Richard Ellsworth Day's *Bush Aglow: The Life Story of Dwight Lyman Moody, Commoner of Northfield* (Philadelphia: The Judson Press, 1936), 128.
2. A. W. Tozer, *The Fire of God's Presence*, 75.
3. Frank Bartleman, *How Pentecost Came to Los Angeles*, 97–98.
4. Ibid., 19–20.

CHAPTER 17

Impartation

Now, who is going to trust God for the winged life?
You can crawl instead if you wish. God will even
bless you if you crawl; He will do the best He can for
you, but oh how much better to avail ourselves of
our wonderful privileges in Christ and to "mount up
with wings as eagles, run and not be weary, walk and
not faint." O beloved friends, there is a life on wings.
I feel the streams of His life fill me and permeate
my mortal frame from my head to my feet, until no
words are adequate to describe it. I can only make
a few bungling attempts to tell you what it is like
and ask the Lord to reveal to you the rest. May He
reveal to you your inheritance in Christ Jesus so that
you will press on and get all that He has for you.[1]

—CARRIE JUDD MONTGOMERY

Impartation is when someone who has experienced breakthrough or favor in one area releases that same blessing for breakthrough over you. It accelerates your growth. When Moses laid his hands on Joshua, great wisdom was imparted (Deuteronomy 34:9).[2] When someone who has favor on his or her life for finances, healing, words of knowledge, faith, or any other thing prays for you to receive that same blessing, this is called impartation. They freely give away what they have freely received (Matthew 10:8). Although it's always great to have hands laid upon you, you can still receive healing and impartation without being physically present (Matthew 8:5–13; Numbers 11:24–26).

Receiving a prayer of impartation is a beautiful thing, but if there's no action that follows it, it might not go very far. For example, if you want to grow in having more anointing to pray for healing for others, and a healing evangelist releases a prayer of impartation over you, that's amazing. But if you then never step out in faith to pray, that impartation won't really make much of an impact. You must activate that new anointing for healing you just received by taking risks in that area to pray for the sick. Impartation and activation must go together to accelerate your growth to the fullest measure.

I pray that as you receive the following prayers of impartation for fasting, you then also marry these with action. If you do so, watch out, because your world is about to be turned upside down for the glory of God.

Prayers of Impartation for the Journey

From the grace I have upon my life to embrace a lifestyle of consistent fasting, I now release that same grace over your life. I pray that as you embark on this journey deeper into the heart of God, the momentum of heaven would be behind you and you would recognize the cloud of witnesses cheering you on (see Hebrews 12:1–2). I pray that even in your first attempt of fasting for fire, there would be a reignition that takes place in your heart. I pray that in your act of consecrating yourself before the Lord through fasting, the reward will always be deeper encounters with Jesus.

As you set yourself aside to focus wholeheartedly on Jesus, may you experience His love in greater measures. May you be perfectly positioned to enter into the feast with the Bridegroom. I loose divine revelations, encounters, and radical union with God as you set out to feast upon Him alone. May God impart the gift of hunger to you so that it is easy to set yourself aside for the sole purpose of communing more deeply with Him. May you be ravished by His love like never before and in turn be inspired to seek Him in more desperate measures.

May fasting for fire help position you to see the face of Jesus and know Him more closely than ever before. As you lock eyes with the One your heart desires most, may you be overwhelmed in His glory. May the fruit of this union be radical love. May you see the kingdom of God break out and be birthed from your life in profound new ways as you set yourself aside to feast upon Him. May you embrace a lifestyle of fasting to feast upon God. May you be launched into your destiny beyond what you could have ever dreamed of. May the fire of His love burn so brightly within you that it causes you to ignite revival fires wherever you go. I pray and declare this over your life in Jesus' name. Amen.

Now, also receive these prayers of impartation from other mothers and fathers in the faith as you step out in your fasting journey.

Heidi Baker prays this over you:

> Lord, I pray as each one pushes away food, whether it's meats and sweets or whatever kind of fasting it is, that You put truth around their waist. During their times away from the throng, away from the crowds, away from it all, may their minds be protected with a powerful helmet of salvation's full deliverance so that there are no lies, in Jesus' name. May they take "the mighty razor-sharp Spirit-sword of the spoken Word of God" (Ephesians 6:18 TPT).

When they spend the time they normally would spend on preparing and eating food to instead feast upon You, strengthen them. As these push aside food, media, distraction in response to Your call to separate themselves for a season of fasting and prayer, separate them fully and totally to You. Thank You, God, that their hearts are protected and covered with Your armor. Thank You that You strengthen their minds as they fast. Thank You, God, for each one as they step into this place of fasting and prayer.

May You make their feet run like deer's feet.

Thank You, Jesus. Amen.

Lou Engle prays over you:

Father, I pray for this company who are reading this right now, for the inward grace of fasting to come upon them. I pray that You would hotly pursue them. Don't leave them alone. Hunt them down, God.

Like the great missionary martyr to the Auca Indians, Jim Elliot, said, "Am I ignitable, God? Let me not sink to be a clog. Make me Thy fuel, flame of God. Deliver me from the dread asbestos of other things." Asbestos doesn't burn. God, deliver us from the things that are not consumed. Deliver us from the things that don't burn and that keep us from burning.

God, You said, "You shall love the Lord your God with all your heart, mind and soul and strength" (see Mark 12:30). Lord, would You put that burn in each one of our hearts? As an older man, I don't want to lose my fire. Keep me fasting for the fire.

And right now, as you are reading this, I want you to stretch out your hands and say out loud, "I stretch out my heart and I lay hold of it. Lord, mark me with a Nazirite burn, one that You could say, 'He or she was a burning and shining lamp.'"

Father, right now I loose this grace of fasting. Even as John the Baptist was a friend of the Bridegroom because he was a fasting man, I pray that You would make those who are reading this friends of the Bridegroom. You said, "I no longer call you servants; I call you friends that I share with. And everything the Father tells Me, I make it known to you" (see John 15:15).

As these ones step into fasting for fire, birth assignments, bring them their job descriptions, deliver them from certain temptations and addictions. God, You said, "This kind goeth not out but by prayer and fasting" (Matthew 17:21 KJV). *Father, I'm asking You to release a supernatural encounter in fasting. If they don't get it right away, let them not despise it but hold on to it, knowing that You will reward them publicly. Even with this book, Fasting for Fire, mark men and women for the rest of their lives. In Jesus' name, amen.*

Now It's Your Turn

Now that you have learned all about the gift of fasting and have received impartation, it's time to activate the anointing you have received. There really would be no point in writing a book about fasting without inviting you to taste and see and experience it for yourself. No matter where your starting point is, I encourage you to embrace and integrate Fasting for Fire into your spiritual journey.

I invite you now to take the first step and join me by fasting one day this week. I believe that your simple "yes" to go on this journey together in feasting upon God will ignite a fresh fire within you. I feel that even your attempt to fast one day, whether or not you make it the whole day, will unlock something in your heart that will set things in motion for a radical life full of the Spirit. I believe that fasting will bring alignment in your life in more ways than one and increased acceleration into your destiny.

I encourage you to journal about your experience of stepping into the fire of fasting, give yourself lots of grace, and never give up.

You don't have to go on this journey alone. Join us in fasting on Mondays (or another day that works for you) for our regular and corporate times of fasting together. Then try fasting one day a week each week for a month.

To help catalyze you on your journey, I have included four activations for you to try out one day a week for the next month or as you feel led. May the fire in your heart be sustained in continued fasting.

Will you take the first step and commit to fasting one day this week with me? He's drawing you deeper. The invitation is extended to you.

Will you say "yes"?

Notes

1. Carrie Judd Montgomery, "Life on Wings: The Possibilities of Pentecost," *Triumphs of Faith* 32:8 (August 1912), 171–174. The article was taken from an address Carrie delivered at the Stone Church in Chicago in 1910. The article was first printed in *The Latter Rain Evangel* 3:3 (December 1910), 19–24.

2. The spirit that is upon us can also be transferred and released upon others as well. See Numbers 11:16–17; 2 Kings 2:9.

CHAPTER 18

Activation 1:
The Fire Fast of Intimacy

I believe your "yes" to step into fasting will have ripple effects for eternity. If you have made it this far in the book, well done. The ride is about to get wild. As you begin your fasting journey, or reframe it in the light of His fire and love, I encourage you to set aside Monday or another day this week to embrace the Fire Fast of Intimacy. After eating dinner Sunday night, try to wait until dinner Monday night for your next meal. As you abstain from food by not eating breakfast or lunch that day, focus on feasting upon God and deepening your relationship with Him. This fast is all about adoration and worshiping Jesus, the King of kings. I encourage you to adopt this theme for the whole week. Invite friends to join you in this new adventure.

Instead of interceding for others or praying for God to give you things you are contending for (unless led of the Spirit in that direction, of course), when you feel hunger pains, focus your attention and affection upon worshiping Jesus in adoration during this fast. The Fire Fast of Intimacy is not about doing or striving or achieving breakthrough; it's simply about *being* with Jesus, loving Him well, and ministering to *His* heart.

Lean into the Lord. Sit with Him in stillness. Listen to what He wants to whisper to you. Your only agenda for this fast is to seek the face of Jesus, worship Him, and rest in Him. This is communion with God. Throughout the day, pay attention to even the smallest details that are unique or highlighted to you, and make sure to write these down. From this place of intimacy, if God does lead you into prayer, intercession, or some other direction, then follow His lead.

Scripture Meditation and Memorization

I encourage you to specifically read out loud and meditate on the following Scriptures during your fasting day. I also encourage you to memorize Psalm 27:4 this week.

> *Though an army besiege me,*
> *my heart will not fear;*

though war break out against me,
even then I will be confident.
One thing I ask from the Lord,
this only do I seek:
that I may dwell in the house of the Lord
all the days of my life,
to gaze on the beauty of the Lord
and to seek him in his temple (Psalm 27:3–4).
Fasten me upon your heart as a seal of fire
forevermore.
This living, consuming flame
will seal you as my prisoner of love.
My passion is stronger
than the chains of death and the grave,
all consuming as the very flashes of fire
from the burning heart of God.
Place this fierce, unrelenting fire over your entire
being.
Rivers of pain and persecution
will never extinguish this flame.
Endless floods will be unable
to quench this raging fire that burns within you.
Everything will be consumed.
It will stop at nothing
as you yield everything to this furious fire

until it won't even seem to you like a sacrifice anymore (Song of Songs 8:6–7 TPT).

Additional Reading

Read chapter 10, "Intimacy: The Key to Keeping the Flame," in *Ignite Azusa: Positioning for a New Jesus Revolution* by Jennifer A. Miskov.

Read chapter 1, "The Secret Place," and chapter 6, "Focus," in *Walking on Water: Experiencing a Life of Miracles, Courageous Faith and Union with God* by Jennifer A. Miskov.

Questions for Reflection

Before you go to sleep after your day of fasting, journal and answer any of the following questions that are highlighted to you to help you process what God is doing in your heart.

- What words or phrases in the Scriptures for meditation and memorization stood out the most to you and why?

- Was there anything about God's character that was revealed to you in a new way?

- How did it feel having no other agenda than simply to love and minister to Jesus today?

- What did God show you today?

- What patterns or themes were prevalent?

- Did anything unusual or out of the ordinary happen today? Any random phone calls, emails, letters? Any reconnections? Any new ideas or opportunities?

- Are there any action steps God is leading you to take as a response?

- What was the hardest thing about doing the fast?

- Were there any areas of frustration that surfaced? What did God say about the root of these?

- Is there anything else you want to note from your day of fasting?

Remember, in this Fire Fast of Intimacy, you are not fasting to get something out of God or for a certain breakthrough; you are simply fasting to grow closer to Him. If you don't feel anything or it seems like God is silent, don't be discouraged. He is still near whether you have a defining encounter or if this is just a time to still your heart and draw close (see Hebrews 13:5).

The more you practice fasting, the easier it becomes. Celebrate all of your efforts and heart positioning to hunger for more of Him. No matter how far you make it in your fast, He is so proud of you. Fasting is not about accomplishing a goal but about deepening relationship, and there's so much grace.

CHAPTER 19

Activation 2: The Fire Fast of Consecration

Well done on your first week of fasting! For your second activation, set aside Monday or another day this week to embrace the Fire Fast of Consecration. As you abstain from food, focus on feasting upon God and welcoming His refining fire to purify you. This fast is all about allowing God to purify your heart so that you can see Jesus more clearly (see Matthew 5:8). It's about welcoming God to search your heart and remove anything that would hinder you from all that He has for you. It's about embracing a fresh baptism of fire no matter how painful it might be, trusting God is working deeply. It's about letting no impure motive exist.

Silence is a purifying fire. During this day of fasting, spend some time being still before the Lord. Then welcome a fresh baptism of fire over every single area of your life. Welcome His fire to come to your relationships, plans, dreams, struggles, commitments, work, play, finances. Give the Holy Spirit permission to burn away anything that might hold you back from all that God has for you. Welcome God to bring alignment into *every* area of your life. Be courageous to throw off whatever hinders to run the race set before you, fixing your eyes upon Jesus.

Remember, this fast is not about searching for faults or trying to *make* yourself be set apart for God. It's about welcoming a baptism of His fiery presence to consume you and then responding to whatever He brings to the surface. Invite His correction, repent if necessary, then receive His love and forgiveness.

King David articulates a prayer of consecration we can embrace as our own.

> *God, I invite your searching gaze into my heart.*
> *Examine me through and through;*
> *find out everything that may be hidden within me.*
> *Put me to the test and sift through all my anxious cares.*
> *See if there is any path of pain I'm walking on,*

and lead me back to your glorious, everlasting
way—
the path that brings me back to you (Psalm
139:23–24 TPT).

I also encourage you to join me in praying this prayer
out loud over your life today:

Lord, send Your fire over my life today. I trust
You. Remove anything that is causing pain and
is holding me back from all that You have for me.
Lord, send Your fire over every single area of my
life, over every relationship, over all of my plans,
dreams, future hopes. Lord, send Your fire over
all of the challenges I am facing, over all of my
fears, insecurities, failures. Lord, send Your fire
over all of my relationships and commitments,
my work, my family, my destiny, and over all my
thoughts. Lord, come and consume every area.
Let nothing be untouched by Your fire. If there is
anything at all that is not pleasing to You, I give
You permission to burn it away. Only let the gold
remain. Come, Holy Spirit, with a fresh baptism
of fire over my life today. In Jesus' name, amen
and let it be so.

Scripture Meditation and Memorization

I encourage you to specifically read out loud and meditate on the following Scriptures during your fasting day. I also encourage you to memorize Hebrews 12:1–2 this week.

> *Therefore, since we are surrounded by such a great cloud of witnesses, let us throw off everything that hinders and the sin that so easily entangles. And let us run with perseverance the race marked out for us, fixing our eyes on Jesus, the pioneer and perfecter of faith. For the joy set before him he endured the cross, scorning its shame, and sat down at the right hand of the throne of God (Hebrews 12:1–2).*

But now, this is what the Lord says…

> *"Do not fear, for I have redeemed you;*
> *I have summoned you by name; you are mine.*
> *When you pass through the waters,*
> *I will be with you;*
> *and when you pass through the rivers,*
> *they will not sweep over you.*
> *When you walk through the fire,*
> *you will not be burned;*

the flames will not set you ablaze" (Isaiah 43:1–2).

[John the Baptist said,] *"But after me comes one who is more powerful than I, whose sandals I am not worthy to carry. He will baptize you with the Holy Spirit and fire. His winnowing fork is in his hand, and he will clear his threshing floor, gathering his wheat into the barn and burning up the chaff with unquenchable fire"* (Matthew 3:11–12).

Therefore, I urge you, brothers and sisters, in view of God's mercy, to offer your bodies as a living sacrifice, holy and pleasing to God—this is your true and proper worship. Do not conform to the pattern of this world, but be transformed by the renewing of your mind. Then you will be able to test and approve what God's will is— his good, pleasing and perfect will (Romans 12:1–2).

Additional Reading

Read chapter 6, "The Fire Burns Deep," in *Ignite Azusa: Positioning for a New Jesus Revolution* by Jennifer A. Miskov.

Read chapter 4, "The Art of Letting Go," in *Walking on Water: Experiencing a Life of Miracles, Courageous Faith and Union with God* by Jennifer A. Miskov.

Questions for Reflection

- What specific theme or themes did the Lord highlight during this fast?

- Was there anything God told you to get rid of, let go of, or surrender to Him?

- If so, what action steps will you take this week to respond in swift obedience?

- What deeper revelations from your Scripture meditation/memorization did you experience?

- What did you learn the second time around that you didn't the first time? Was there anything different about fasting this time than last time?

- What was your week like following the fast? Did you notice any changes? Did anything unusually Godlike happen?

Remember that whenever God strips something from our lives, it is only because He has something better, and that thing or person is hindering Him from pouring out His full blessings. Lean into the fire, and trust that the Father's intentions are good and that everything He strips away is for your best. He has beautiful things awaiting you, and He needs your arms to be empty so He can come and fill them.

CHAPTER 20

Activation 3:
The Fire Fast of Revival

You're doing great! I hope now after your second fast that you have begun to experience some of the joys of fasting. Now for your third activation, set aside Monday or another day this week to embrace the Fire Fast of Revival. As you abstain from food, focus on feasting upon God and praying for the fire of revival to be ignited in you. Welcome the Holy Spirit to come and resurrect any areas of your own heart that are dead. Ask Him to awaken and stir your heart for the lost. Ask God to break your heart for what breaks His. Ask Him how you can demonstrate His love to those around you. Ask Him to pour out the oil of His Spirit upon you and set you ablaze to be a burning one who will bring the Good News to those around you with great boldness, anointing, and power.

Ask God to show you how you can bring His love to someone around you today, and then step out in boldness to respond as the Spirit leads. No matter what the result might be, our responsibility is obedience. I believe your one act of faith in stepping out to love the one God highlights will unlock something inside of you and set things in motion for a move of God to continue in and through your life.

Scripture Meditation and Memorization

I encourage you to specifically read out loud and meditate on the following Scriptures during your fasting day. I also encourage you to memorize Luke 10:2–3 this week.

> He told them, "The harvest is plentiful, but the workers are few. Ask the Lord of the harvest, therefore, to send out workers into his harvest field. Go! I am sending you out like lambs among wolves" (Luke 10:2–3).
>
> Is not this the kind of fasting I have chosen:
> to loose the chains of injustice
> and untie the cords of the yoke,
> to set the oppressed free
> and break every yoke?

Is it not to share your food with the hungry
and to provide the poor wanderer with shelter—
when you see the naked, to clothe them,
and not to turn away from your own flesh and
blood?
Then your light will break forth like the dawn,
and your healing will quickly appear;
then your righteousness will go before you,
and the glory of the Lord will be your rear guard.
Then you will call, and the Lord will answer;
you will cry for help, and he will say: Here am I
(Isaiah 58:6–9).

Additional Reading

Read chapter 3, "The Azusa Story," in *Ignite Azusa: Positioning for a New Jesus Revolution* by Jennifer A. Miskov.

Read chapter 16, "Courage," in *Walking on Water: Experiencing a Life of Miracles, Courageous Faith and Union with God* by Jennifer A. Miskov.

Questions for Reflection

- What stood out or was highlighted most to you during your fast today and why?

- Did He put a specific person on your heart today in a new way and, if so, did He show you why this person was brought to mind?
- Did He give you any ideas of ways to demonstrate His love for another person?
- How did/will you respond to what He revealed to you today?
- How do you feel after stepping out in faith in response to His leading?

Way to lean into your third fast! God is softening your heart and drawing you closer to Him every step of the way. I am right here with you cheering you on.

CHAPTER 21

Bonus Activation 4: The Fire Fast of Destiny

While our truest destiny is being in love with Jesus, there are also specific assignments for us to fulfill in our lifetime that God has prepared beforehand for us to walk in. This extra activation will be to do a Fire Fast of Destiny. Set aside Monday or another day this week to fast. As you abstain from food, focus on feasting upon God and praying for deeper revelation of the specific assignments in this season that God has called you to fulfill. Ask God to resurrect dreams, promises, and seeds that He has planted that have died or become dormant within you. Ask Him to awaken you to your true destiny.

God has already gone before you and planted certain dreams and desires within you that only you can walk out.

You are not trying to make something happen through striving but are leaning into God's heart to have Him reveal what has already been planted inside of you. You are learning how to partner with heaven in the God-given calling and assignments specific to you.

We are naturally launched into our destinies through intimacy with Jesus and connection with the family of God. As you dive deeper into your relationship with Jesus through fasting and get more connected with the tribe of burning ones He has positioned you to run with in this season, you will be launched into a greater measure of your destiny.

Scripture Meditation and Memorization

I encourage you to specifically read out loud and meditate on the following Scriptures during your fasting day. I also encourage you to memorize one of the Ephesians 2:10 versions that most resonates with you this week.

> For we are God's masterpiece. He has created us anew in Christ Jesus, so we can do the good things he planned for us long ago (Ephesians 2:10 NLT).
>
> We have become his poetry, a re-created people that will fulfill the destiny he has given each

of us, for we are joined to Jesus, the Anointed One. Even before we were born, God planned in advance our destiny and the good works we would do to fulfill it! (Ephesians 2:10 TPT)

For we are God's handiwork, created in Christ Jesus to do good works, which God prepared in advance for us to do (Ephesians 2:10 NIV).

For we are His workmanship, created in Christ Jesus for good works, which God prepared beforehand that we should walk in them (Ephesians 2:10 NKJV).

Now to Him who is able to do exceedingly abundantly above all that we ask or think, according to the power that works in us, to Him be glory in the church by Christ Jesus to all generations, forever and ever. Amen (Ephesians 3:20–21 NKJV).

Therefore, my dear brothers and sisters, stand firm. Let nothing move you. Always give yourselves fully to the work of the Lord, because you know that your labor in the Lord is not in vain (1 Corinthians 15:58 NIV).

Additional Reading

Read chapter 12, "The Opportunity of a Lifetime Is at Our Door," in *Ignite Azusa: Positioning for a New Jesus Revolution* by Jennifer A. Miskov.

Read chapter 9, "It Was Not Jesus' Idea," and chapter 13, "Miracle Flight," in *Walking on Water: Experiencing a Life of Miracles, Courageous Faith and Union with God* by Jennifer A. Miskov.

Read *Silver to Gold: A Journey of Young Revolutionaries* by Jennifer A. Miskov.

Questions for Reflection

- What was highlighted for you in the Scripture meditation and why?

- What dreams or seeds did God resurrect in your life during this fast?

- What did God reveal to you about your specific calling and assignments?

- What practical steps will you take this week to invest into the dreams and assignments God has placed within you?

- Is there anything you are carrying that is not in alignment with your God-given destiny and assignments? If so, what will you do this week to position yourself to fully step into all that God has called you to for such a time as this?

Bonus Reflection Questions After Fasting Once a Week for a Month

- How has your life changed by adopting fasting as a lifestyle this month?
- Moving forward, how often will you now integrate fasting into your spiritual walk?
- What will that look like for you?
- What has been your biggest takeaway from this month of fasting?

Congratulations on going all in! I believe your willingness to set yourself apart to burn for Jesus is honored by all of heaven. I am so grateful that you decided to join me on this journey; it has been such an honor to run alongside you. I hope that you have not only discovered the benefits of fasting but have also experienced them too.

I have great news for you. This journey doesn't have to end here. Consider now adopting a *lifestyle* of fasting for fire and invite your friends to join you. And let's continue to burn!

CHAPTER 22

Bonus Tips

(Adapted from
Digging the Wells of Revival)

by Lou Engle

Effective Fasting and Prayer[1]

Perhaps you've never fasted or you've fasted for only a meal here and there. Let me share some thoughts with you from my experiences, and those of others, so that you may be helped and encouraged and may receive the most from your wonderful obedience.

1. *Fast and pray to humble yourself and to purify your worship.*

Remember, the purpose of fasting is to align your heart with God's heart. We are not trying to get something from

God but are seeking to realign our hearts' affection with His. To do this, we must do "holy violence to" the "pleasures that wage war" against the soul (see Mathew 11:12 and James 4:1 NASB). We must open a way for the Holy Spirit's passion to dominate us. In fasting, we can more readily say, "We love You, Lord, more than anything in the world." Lust of any kind perverts worship but fasting enables us to cleanse the sanctuary of our hearts of every other rival. As was true in Daniel's fast, the dominant emphasis must be on humility and confession, not the object we seek.

2. Take time to pray and to read the Word.

This may seem obvious, but busyness and distractions abound. What is the use of opening yourself to more of God, of His revelation, and of insight in His Word if you don't avail yourself of them? Remember, this is a time when you can hear and respond more clearly—and often more powerfully—and can enjoy the presence and glory of God in a special way. Don't miss out on it!

3. Have a clear target for prayer focus.

Without a vision (a clear, prophetic prayer goal), people perish (Proverbs 29:19). During a fast, I often pray into four or five prayer goals, but I must make sure that they are clearly articulated. When I'm not deeply motivated by a clear goal, I usually fast until break-fast! Write down the vision so you can run with it (Habakkuk 2:2).

4. Do the fast with someone else.

Two are better than one. If one falls, the other picks him up (Ecclesiastes 4:9–10). Perhaps you have a prayer partner. Many years back, I completed a forty-day season of prayer and fasting with a prayer partner to re-dig the wells of revival in Los Angeles. As part of our time together, we read the account of Frank Bartleman praying with William Boehmer. By praying and fasting with a partner, you may be more motivated to pray and fast for your goal.

5. Do not give in to condemnation if you fail.

The "fast or not to fast" schizophrenia can be a major tool of the enemy. Even though you may fail several times, God always extends grace. Hit reset and resume right where you left off. The Lord will give you fresh motivation. I remember one fast where I gave up and sneaked some yogurt and chips. The next day an intercessor came to me and said, "I saw you in a dream. You were supposed to be fasting, but you were eating yogurt and chips." That was pretty good motivation to start again—and to realize that what I was doing must be of some significance!

6. Make your commitment and determine the length of your fast.

People often report that fasting is easier the longer you go. Historically, the most significant results have come through extended fasts at the Lord's leading.

- A total fast is without water. Don't go beyond three days.

- A water-only fast is very difficult but very effective. Depending on your weight and metabolism, you may go up to forty days on water.

- A fruit and vegetable juice fast allows you to enter into the spirit of fasting but still gives energy. Most people can do a forty-day juice fast. For this fast, drink small amounts of low-acidic or nonacidic juices. This gives you the desired effect of fasting but also gives your body strength and needed minerals. Apple, cranberry, and watermelon juices are excellent, as is vegetable broth. It is best to schedule your juice intake. To drink juice continually may hinder the spirit of fasting and self-control. An undiluted juice fast is much easier and is still very beneficial. For many people, it may help to drink protein drinks. This is especially advisable if you have health and/or weight considerations. Out of consideration for their health and metabolism, I encourage teenagers to drink juice and protein drinks to sustain them.

- A Daniel fast of vegetables and water is good for those employed in manual labor or for those who carry a heavy workload (like moms).
- A milkshake fast isn't really a fast!

7. *Prepare physically.*

Limit your intake of food to fruit and vegetables for two days before an extended fast. Fruit is a natural cleanser and is easy to digest. If you can, stop drinking coffee several days before you fast. Prepare yourself for mental discomforts such as impatience, crankiness, and anxiety. Expect physical discomforts. You may experience dizziness, headaches, and different pains. The headaches are not a sign to stop fasting. Your body is working to cleanse itself of impurities.

8. *Prepare for opposition.*

Satan tempted Jesus during His fast, and we must expect the same. You can bet that someone will bring donuts to the office on the day of your fast. It is amazing how this works! Your spouse may suddenly be inspired to cook your favorite meals for the rest of the family. *Press through.* You may also feel tension build in your home. Work through this with your spouse. My fasts are just as difficult for my wife as they are for me. She, too, must be well prepared before I begin to fast. Likewise, discouragement may seek to overtake you like a flood. Recognize the source of the discouragement and stand on the victory of Christ.

9. Fast in secret.

Don't boast about your fast, but don't be afraid to let people know before you go to their homes that you won't be eating.

10. Break the fast gradually.

On an extended fast of light juice or water, your digestive system shuts down completely. This can pose a great danger if you are not careful. So as not to harm your body, you must exercise strong self-control when you begin to break the fast. Begin with several days of diluted, nonacidic juice. Then take regular strength juice and vegetable broth for several days. After a week, you may begin to drink light non-milk soups and thicker juices like V8, carrot juice, and green vegetable juices. Fruit and vegetables may follow. I broke too quickly after one of my early fasts and nearly needed hospitalization. Be careful!

11. Feel free to rest much and to engage in light exercise.

12. Seek medical advice and oversight before and during the fast if you have medical problems or are older. If you are pregnant or nursing, do not fast—period. Consider doing a social media or TV fast instead.

13. Expect to hear God's voice through dreams, visions, revelations, and the Word.

Daniel prepared himself to receive revelation through fasting (Daniel 10:1–2). Prepare yourself in a similar manner, focusing on your goal and making sure that you understand what God is wanting to do. Then fast expectantly. God has promised that He will reward you (Matthew 6:18). I heard a story that while ministering in Malaysia, a brother was "caught up into the heavens" during a forty-day fast. After the fast, he took a team into the interior of Borneo, where he saw a dead woman raised and revival break out in a village!

14. Don't be discouraged if you don't see immediate results. Many times, breakthroughs come after a fast—sometimes long after.

Do not listen to the lies that nothing is happening. It is my conviction that God rewards every person who fasts in faith. When Jesus was baptized by John, the heavens opened and the dove descended upon Him. Immediately thereafter, that same dove drove Him into the wilderness to fast for forty days and to contend with the territorial strongman over the earth, satan himself. For forty days, Jesus warred through prayer and fasting to reverse the curse of Adam and Eve and to overcome the devil and release atomic power into the earth. The results recorded in Luke show that history changed forever through the strength and victory the Lord gained by His obedience. Divine power was now His! "Jesus returned to Galilee in the *power* of the Spirit, and news about Him spread through the whole countryside" (Luke 4:14).

On the other hand, the Israelites spent *forty years* in the wilderness complaining about food and yearning to go back to the leeks and garlic of Egypt. They preferred captivity to the discipline of the wilderness. America is in the wilderness right now. Our choice is this: Do we prefer captivity under the territorial strongmen that hold sway over our cities, our neighborhoods, and our loved ones? Or will we pray and fast until the curse of evil is removed from our land and the wells of revival are re-dug? If we want *apostolic results* like the power Jesus exercised, we must return to *apostolic methods*. It's our choice—forty years or forty days!

Note

1. Adapted from chapter 11, "Atomic Power Through Prayer and Fasting," in Lou Engle's *Digging the Wells of Revival: Reclaiming Your Historic Inheritance Through Prophetic Intercession* (Shippensburg, PA: Destiny Image Publishers, 1998). Used with permission from the publisher. See also https://thejesusfast.global/resources.

Further Resources

Baker, Rolland and Heidi. *There's Always Enough* (England: Sovereign World Ltd, 2003). Heidi talks about the encounter she had that defined her calling while on a fast.

Bankus, John K. *Fasting Outside the Box: Fasting Guidelines for Beginners* (Bloomington, IN: Westbow Press, 2013). I like this book because it puts fasting into the context of relationship with Jesus. I met this author at Home of Peace one day, and he told me how reading my book *Spirit Flood: Rebirth of Spirit Baptism for the 21st Century* encouraged him and also inspired him to write this book.

Bartleman, Frank. *How Pentecost Came to Los Angeles: As It Was in the Beginning,* 2nd edition (Los Angeles, CA: Frank Bartleman, originally published in 1925). Bartleman was not only a historian who captured the beginnings of the Azusa Street Revival; he also prayed and fasted to partner with God to see a great move of God take place in Los Angeles.

Engle, Lou. *The Fast: Rediscovering Jesus' Pathway to Power* (Colorado Springs, CO: Engle House Publishing, 2020) and Lou Engle with Dean Briggs, *Jesus Fast* (Bloomington, MN: Chosen Books, 2016). I don't know of many people today who have paved the way in prayer and fasting for this generation to return to God as much as this man has.

Grubb, Norman P. *Rees Howells: Intercessor* (Fort Washington, PA: CLC Publications, 2008, reprint from Lutterworth Press in England 1952). This is a biography about the consecrated life of Rees Howells.

Foster, Richard. *Celebration of Discipline: The Path to Spiritual Growth* (New York, NY: HarperOne, 1978, reprint 1998). This is a great foundational book that covers the spiritual disciplines.

Habib, Samaa and Bodie Thoene. *Face to Face with Jesus* (Bloomington, MN: Chosen Books, 2014). Samaa is a personal friend who regularly does longer fasts and is set apart as a burning one in love with Jesus. Her story told in this book is quite remarkable.

Hall, Franklin. *Atomic Power with God Through Fasting and Prayer* (Phoenix, AZ, new edition 1973). This is a book that Lou Engle told me about that marked his life.

Johnson, Bill with Jennifer A. Miskov. *Defining Moments: God Encounters with Ordinary People Who Changed the World* (New Kensington, PA: Whitaker House, 2016). This book is filled with encounters and revival movements that were birthed when people were on a fast.

Martin, Lee Roy. *Fasting: A Centre for Pentecostal Theology Short Introduction* (Cleveland, TN: CPT Press, 2014). Written by a friend and colleague of mine. I like this book because it is very thorough in looking at fasting throughout Scripture. It also traces fasting in some areas of revival history. The references to further works on fasting are also helpful.

McPherson, Aimee Semple. *This Is That: Personal Experiences, Sermons and Writings of Aimee Semple McPherson* (Los Angeles, CA: The Bridal Call Publishing House, 1919). This will give you deeper insights into McPherson's life and her hunger for the Lord.

Miskov, Jennifer A. *Walking on Water: Experiencing a Life of Miracles, Courageous Faith and Union with God* (Bloomington, MN: Chosen Books, 2017). This is the first real book where I share my personal story. I share more in-depth about what happened after my forty-day fast and the breakthrough of Destiny House that followed.

Miskov, Jennifer A. with Heidi Baker, Lou Engle, and Bill Johnson. *Ignite Azusa: Positioning for a New Jesus Revolution* (Redding, CA: Silver to Gold, 2016). This is all about the Azusa Street Revival as well as consecration and a prayer for a fresh baptism of fire.

Prince, Derek. *Shaping History Through Prayer and Fasting* (New Kensington, PA: Whitaker House, 1973, 2002). This is the book that Lou Engle referred to that shaped his fasting journey.

Towns, Elmer L. *Knowing God Through Fasting* (Shippensburg, PA: Destiny Image, 2002). He writes about how he has grown closer to God through fasting and how that alone makes fasting worth it every time.

Disclaimer

Please be led of the Spirit and also welcome doctors and medical experts into your life if needed to help guide you along this journey in fasting so that you don't unnecessarily harm yourself. You are choosing to step into fasting by your own free will. I also want to warn you that some of the side effects of choosing a lifestyle of fasting might be that your world is turned upside down. You may have a closer relationship with God, experience greater alignment in your destiny, and move in greater anointing. You are responsible for your actions in regard to fasting, so please be wise and get help if needed.

Acknowledgments

I am so grateful for everyone who encouraged me to get this book out. I had made steps toward releasing this on my own but really needed help in the final push to get it out there. Thanks to Steve Lawson who reminded me that my life is marked with revival and that I needed to integrate this theme into the book to give it a unique flavor. I am extremely grateful for Larry Sparks and the Destiny Image family for immediately being so excited and willing to publish my manuscript. It was Larry who had the brilliant idea to get Lou Engle's voice included here. I am also grateful for Lou Engle's "yes" to partnering with me in this book. It was our mutual passion for re-digging the wells of revival that initially brought us together years ago at Carrie Judd Montgomery's Home of Peace in Oakland while Lou was on a forty-day fast. I am humbled by his life laid down to fast and pray to see a generation burn with the fire of God.

I want to thank Heidi Baker, not only for her contributions to this work, but also for believing in me and championing the call of God on my life consistently now for over two decades. I definitely would not be where I am today without her example of being a burning lover of Jesus and her belief in me. She is one of the most resilient and determined people I know and has played a huge role in so many of my personal breakthroughs. I am also grateful to Randy Clark for bringing his perspective and experience of fasting to the table. What God has released through his life on the other side of fasting is powerful. He walks with great humility and is such a tremendous gift to the body of Christ.

I am so grateful to Jessica Lewis for reading through this manuscript multiple times and giving some very insightful and timely feedback that helped shape this work. She was a true lifesaver in the process! Thanks also to Sharon Tuemmler for doing an extra edit to bless me and also to Lauren Stinton for jumping on board to help in the editorial process toward the end. I am thankful to the whole team at Destiny Image for their investment into this project. Special thanks to Eileen Rockwell for her amazing cover design, John Martin for helping bring this project to life, Tammy for her editing, and all the others on the team who have sown their gifts and talents into bringing this work to life.

I am also grateful to the entire School of Revival family who all championed, believed in, encouraged, and covered me in prayer for this birth. I want to thank Tremonisha Putros, Gabby Heusser, and the Writing in the Glory family for their faithful prayers and for keeping me motivated to complete this project! Special thanks to my beautiful revivalist friend and fellow faster, Jessi Green, for consistently encouraging me in my writing and for living a life of fire. The fruit that has come from her life as a result of fasting is inspiring and has impacted me and our region in a profound way.

I want to thank my mom and dad for all of their encouragement, prayers, and support for me during this process. What a joy it has been to have my mom joining me in fasting on Mondays!

To all those who have prayed for, encouraged, and believed in me during this process, I am so grateful. And most importantly, I want to thank the Holy Spirit for anointing me to write this work.

About
Jennifer A. Miskov, Ph.D.

Jennifer A. Miskov, Ph.D., is a revival historian, writing coach, and itinerant minister who loves to lead people into a lifestyle of intimacy with Jesus and invite them to experience the fullness of the Holy Spirit. Through her Writing in the Glory workshops and coaching, Jen enjoys helping revivalist authors birth their first books. During the 2020 pandemic, she launched School of Revival online to equip and raise up revivalists around the world. She is originally from Anaheim, California, and is ordained by Heidi Baker with Iris Global. She received her Ph.D. in Global Pentecostal and Charismatic Studies from the University of Birmingham, U.K. You can learn more at JenMiskov.com.